A CERTAIN STATE OF MIND

First published in 1995 by *Salzburg University*
in its series:
SALZBURG STUDIES IN ENGLISH LITERATURE
POETIC DRAMA & POETIC THEORY
135

EDITOR: JAMES HOGG

ISBN 3-7052-0941-8

INSTITUT FÜR ANGLISTIK UND AMERIKANISTIK
UNIVERSITÄT SALZBURG
A-5020 SALZBURG
AUSTRIA

Cover design by Robert W. Palmer incorporates *Soldiers in Time of Peace*, a woodcut by Hokusai. Courtesy of Ulysses Bookshop.

James Kirkup asserts his right to be regarded as the author of all the material in this book.

A CERTAIN STATE OF MIND

An Anthology of Classic, Modern and
Contemporary Japanese Haiku in Translation
with Essays and Reviews

by

JAMES KIRKUP

UNIVERSITY OF SALZBURG
1995

In Memory

of the five great masters
of modern haiku —

Mizuhara Shūōshi	(1892-1981)
Takano Sujū	(1893-1976)
Awano Seiho	(1899-1993)
Yamaguchi Seishi	(1901-1994)
and	
Katō Shūson	(1905-1993)

CONTENTS

PREFACE : A CERTAIN STATE OF MIND

Haiku are not poems. At least, they are not poems in the sense that we in the West think of poetry. For us, the word "poem" brings to mind a usually long, carefully-constructed work: even the briefest poems in western languages have a certain willed quality as well as — if the poet is lucky — true poetical inspiration. So the word "poem" raises our expectations very high. And when we are confronted, perhaps for the first time, by the shortness and compactness of haiku, we can hardly believe that these three lines of seventeen syllables can really be classed under the heading of "poetry" or even "light verse".

Yet these brief flashes of illumination from the haiku poet's heart and mind as he confronts the phenomena, both natural and artificial, of our one and only world are poems in their own right. They have simply been conceived in a different way from western works. The haiku poet has cast a different, oblique eye at our daily life and listened with a differently-tuned ear to the immortal whisperings in every human soul. That eye and ear belong to the universal language of all poetry, in whatever language it is written. Just because it is different from what we expect of poetry does not disqualify it in the ranks of literary skill and feeling when it is composed with the skill and seriousness of a true *haijin*. It is we who are mistaken if we dismiss it out of hand as merely "light-weight" or "lacking in substance".

For the art of haiku, if the art is to succeed in Japanese and in any language, requires *a certain state of mind*, a predisposition to be surprised by the ordinary things and events which we normally ignore in our busy and often empty daily lives. The haiku requires our own goodwill, a desire to enter freely into its other world of art that is in fact the art of living. Centuries of civilization have become absorbed in the haiku that takes one second to conceive and one minute to write down.

(From the Preface to A FIRST BIRD SINGING by Katō Kōko, translated by James Kirkup and Katō Kōko, Hub Editions 1993 (ISBN 1 870653 23 8)).

INTRODUCTION

The first section in this anthology contains translations of modern and classical haiku associated with a collection of *shikishi* (square poem cards), *tanzaku* (long narrow poem cards) and *kakemono* (poem scrolls) donated by the Museum of Haiku Literature in Tokyo to the British Haiku Society in London, where they are to be seen from time to time at Daiwa Japan House, 13-14 Cornwall Terrace, NW1 4QP. The exhibition is also intended for display in schools and other suitable places throughout Britain.

Nearly all the haiku obey the traditional 5-7-5-syllable form, and so do my translations, with a few exceptions that prove the rule, for Japanese poets also sometimes write in freer forms. For example, the haiku of Kaneko Tōta has 8-7-6 syllables, so I have tried to respect his construction in English.

The rest of the anthology contains haiku chosen at random, and they are not arranged in any special order, though occasionally two or three with the same seasonal theme come together. All the originals are in 17-syllable form, and have the season word that acts as a kind of anchor in the composition of this kind of verse. Today, some *haijin* write haiku without a season word, but my own feeling is that this particular reference to a certain time of year is an essential element in haiku that are for the most part about the natural phenomena and human reactions to them. Most of them are modern and contemporary, with a few classical.

There is an astonishing range of themes, some of them unlike anything ever found before in western poetry. They seek to interpret the diversity of the whole of Japanese life and thought, and through such perceptions of reality achieve universal dimensions. Even those that at first sight seem most casual and banal reveal, on closer thought, a kind of imagination and a rhythmical resonance of unusual depth.

Three or four poets have been given more extended representation in individual sequences, though their work also appears from time to time in the general order or disorder of the compilation. I have inserted a few prose sections of my own about such subjects as photography (by Willy Ronis) or cinematography (by Robert Bresson) as well as obituaries of four of the major poets which appeared in "The Independent" newspaper in London — the first time obituaries of Japanese haiku poets had ever appeared in the British press. A final section of the book presents haiku essays on various European, Chinese, Catalan, South American and American poets. The recent upsurge of haiku compositions from Romania, Croatia and other Eastern European countries must wait for the next volume for full treatment. They represent a truly remarkable development in the history of haiku.

Much of the work in the presnt volume appeared in "Modern Poetry in Translation" (Iowa), "KO" International Haiku Magazine (Nagoya), "Modern Haiku" (Madison, USA), "Haiku Quarterly" (Swindon, England) and the organ of the British Haiku Society, "Blithe Spirit" (Shalford, England).

In my interpretations of these haiku, I am greatly indebted to Katō Kōko and Tamaki Makoto for their advice and assistance.

I offer my grateful thanks to all the poets, editors and publishers concerned. Unfortunately it was not possible to include the original texts in Japanese.

James Kirkup

(President, the British Haiku Society)

PICTURES FROM AN EXHIBITION

A Suite for Haiku

Great Wall of China --—
this time I came to visit
apricot blossoms

Matsuzaki Tetsunosuke

Sometimes towering
over the ship, the high seas
of an April month

Suzuki Masajo

Strong gusts blowing past —
I found myself muttering
"The winds of Autumn"

Mori Sumio

After the branches
have been pruned away, the sun
gains renewed power

Morita Tōge

Spring sunlight broken
by the ocean waves into
glittering fragments

Inahata Teiko

Birds in migration —
I feel I am rapidly
becoming smaller

Ueda Gosengoku

There is just this much
in a single handful from
the field of horsetails

Kiyosaki Toshio

What was once a white
peony has now become
the moon peony

Kamikura Utsuwa

With the sun shining
everything rejoices —
fruits of the *nandin*

Hoshino Bakkyūjin

1

Touched by the sunlight —
the mountain's seven colours —
bracken coming out   Okada Nichio

Everyday mind
in everyday clothing —
the peach tree blossoms   Hosomi Ayako

I am just one of
a flock of sheep, receiving
the year's first sunlight   Sawaki Kinichi

As one just pops up
one disappears — the dabchicks
always the same count   Naruse Ōtōshi

The graves of the soldiers —
even in death, in the cold,
falling into line   Yamazaki Hisao

While reading a book about cranes
I hang my shirts out to dry on
Himalayan cedars   Kaneko Tōta

All the length and breadth
of Mount Fuji spreading out
over summer fields   Katsura Nobuko

Alone in springtime —
javelin throw — then the walk
to the javelin   Nomura Toshirō

As if obedient
to the power of his will,
thin ice still in spring   Murata Osamu

Back in my home town
there is a transparent sky —
the wild geese crossing   Nakasone Yasuhiro

The first bush clover
is already hanging down
to the stone pathway   Furutachi Sōjin

A wandering monk
striding like a strong wind — one
hundred birds chirping   Fujita Shōshi

With just one finger
tip, the whole pond, covered in
thin ice, can be moved   Gotō Hinao

Wherever I go,
the eyes are following me —
a cat with kittens   Hoshino Tsunehiko

The routes taken by
these trickles of sweat —
these are also words   Takaha Shugyō

TEN CLASSIC HAIKU

Come over here and
let us go play together,
motherless sparrow   Issa

A child is crying,
asking: "Get it down for me!"
— the full moon hanging   Issa

Well — is this to be
my home at life's end, buried
in five feet of snow?   Issa

Skinny little frog,
don't let yourself be beaten —
Issa's on your side!   Issa

I wrote "One person" —
the register at the inn —
chilly autumn night   Issa

Frog jumping into
the stillness of an old pond —
a sound of water   Bashō

At Mokuboji
a tanka-making session —
the August full moon   Kikaku

How interesting!
Hard to recognize at once
garden pampas grass!   Onitsura

Kirigamine —
I look back at the peak — green
grass resurrected   Kakimori

The buckwheat field is
white even in the midnight —
the white moon hanging   Shiki

WILLY RONIS : PHOTOGRAPHER OF HAIKU MOMENTS

Ronis is one of my favourite modern photographers. Like Robert Doisneau, he has photographed mainly Paris street scenes and provincial French towns, but he has also taken magnificent portraits of New York, Prague, Leningrad and other European sites. His latest exhibition at the Hôtel de Sully, Paris, ran from 16 June to 14 September, 1994. He wrote a remarkable introduction to it, which contains some thoughts that can also be applied to the art of haiku.

"...While there are days when subjects are offered you on a platter, there are numerous occasions when you can see nothing, not because there *is* nothing but because you are missing what is there. Therefore this occupation is far from being child's play: it demands concentration, and solitude, and it is based, as far as I'm concerned, on a refusal of the picturesque, the exceptional. I even distrust anything very unusual, so much so that when I get home I often find myself with an empty camera."

These words struck an echo in my mind. Keats in one of his letters writes:

"Poetry should be great and unobtrusive, a thing which enters into one's soul, and does not startle or amaze it with itself, but with its subject."

Ronis goes on to write:

"...What is the true source of this searching? In the familiar, the universal. Not in things that give you a shock of surprise, but in moments of emotion. In the frequent beauty of ordinary life. In fortuitous composition, sometimes overwhelming, of people distributed in a certain space as if by a scenic director of genius. In a radiance that magnifies the banality of the everyday. In the attitudes of protagonists that are not premeditated but which often generate a sense of fulfillment and happiness. In the pursuit, more or less conscious, of a dream of harmony."

5

I think we can learn a lot about how to "see" haiku in everyday life from the example of this great photographer, who recently, at the age of 85, made his third parachute jump (assisted) over Le Bourget, and was holding his camara to register the happy landing. In a recent letter to me, Willy tells me that he took his self-portrait with arms full-length after a free-fall from 3,500 to 1,500 metres. Ronis' work often contains shots taken from a great height. One of his most famous pictures is of two lovers on the narrow balcony at the top of Place de la Bastille column. He tells me that one taken from the top of a ski slope was made with his Minox camera fixed between his skis.

The expression of utter bliss on Willy's face as he landed suggests that the experience was the culmination of a very personal dream, and a truly heavenly vision of the artist's down-to-earth poetic lens.

***

Everyday mind
in everyday clothing —
the peach tree blossoms   Hosomi Ayako

Nightingale warbling
as I continue weaving,
weaving at my loom   Hosomi Ayako

February's end —
my cat has a face for night
and a face for day   Iida Ryūta

Daybreak in springtime —
a young girl, now passed away:
her hair, too, was dark   Iida Ryūta

Such hundreds of them —
swarms of peonies — water
coming to the boil   Mori Sumio

I have travelled so
far — as I realized when
I woke from my nap   Mori Sumio

I saw mountain fires
on Ashigarayama
one night of great grief   Katō Shūson

A smile that faded
away just like an ice floe
slowing to a stop   Katō Shūson

With her squirrel teeth
a young girl all alone
is gnawing a chestnut   Hirahata Seitō

Just saying that spring
is on its way makes the trees
and grasses seem to look so   Issa

The snow has melted:
everywhere in the village
is full of children   Issa

Buddha of flowers
hiding in its heart of hearts
peony's jade bud

Katō Kōko

The peony's bud
of jade undoes its petals
blowing in the wind

Katō Kōko

Everything on earth
contained within the circle
of the rainbow's ring

Yamaguchi Seishi

From the pigeon house
one feather floating up to
the brilliant full moon

Takaha Shugyō

Come outside quickly —
almost close enough to touch,
the moon of springtime

Nakamura Teijô

A fire in the hearth —
flames burning ever brighter
leave us without words

Kaneo Umenomon

Chrysanthemums — cast
as many as we can find
into the coffin

Natsume Sōseki

How beautifully
I danced the Noh in my dream —
winter seclusion

Matsumoto Takashi

In the lotus pond
there is something beating wings
under the full moon

Mizuhara Shūōshi

Arranged in the pot,
gathered deep in the mountains,
magnolia opened

Mizuhara Shūōshi

Woodpecker pecking
hastens the falling of leaves
from the pasture trees

Mizuhara Shūōshi

The ladybird cracks
its wing-case open — begins
fluttering away   Takano Sujū

The wasteland has now
already crept up under
my veranda floor   Kubota Mantarō

On the bare earth left
in the ruins after bombing,
the girls bouncing balls   Nakamura Kusatao

Clearly visible —
star glittering in daylight —
a toadstool growing   Takahama Kyoshi

Autumn wind — breathing
into the open nostrils
of the dead body   Iida Dakotsu

Winter sun, just now
falling upon my eyelids —
how heavy it feels   Takahama Kyoshi

Intravenous drip
drips to all eternity
through the autumn night   Hino Sōjō

Bottle gourd flowers —
moths are flying around
in the falling dusk   Sugita Hisajyo

KINICHI SAWAKI

Between gaps in roads'
iron plates, summer grasses
shooting heavenwards

The red slices of
watermelon tightly sealed
under a glass case

To the white peach
from the darkness of Nara
come striped mosquitos

Kaminoyama —
apples begin to take on
the tints of nipples

Farmer's wife cutting
rice — the water soaks even
as far as her twat

A child is feeding
the petals of the roses
to a ladybird

Spring is almost here —
I used the snow to wipe off
the mud on my shoes

The footsteps sounding
in falling leaves — as of my
dead friend returning

I am like one of
a flock of sheep, receiving
the year's first sunlight

An old woman left
all alone to tend the fire
at the salt-parching

A child already
knows at the end of the snowfield
lies a slaughterhouse

Pulling out a thread
in one long string, the cocoon
has started dancing

***

The blossoms fallen,
it becomes just a temple
among cherry trees   Buson

Nearly sunset, but
still pheasant shooting echoes
round the spring mountains   Buson

When I pinch the wings
of this butterfly, it feels
like nothing on earth   Buson

Mountain-burning fires
are lighting a small night boat
floating downriver   Issa

In the old village
I deserted, the cherry
is now in full bloom   Issa

A girl tea-picker
putting on her sedge hat peeps
in the looking glass   Kagami Shikō

You double-blossomed
cherries, let but one petal fall —
but one petal each   Masaoka Shiki

From days long ago
handcarved *hina* doll — its face
has a knowing look   Mizuhara Shūōshi

The windbell silent —
but the ticking of the clock
makes it feel hotter   Yokoi Yayū

A woman bathing
in a tub in the garden
ogled by a crow   Takahama Kyoshi

The husband and guest
keep sitting in silence with
white chrysanthemums   Ōshima Ryōta

The horsetail grasses
in a jar, caught by sunset
as if in the fields   Ōno Rinka

Whiteness of shollet
that has just been freshly washed
by this cold morning   Bashō

On a wintry sea
the floating seagulls looking
like fallen blossoms   Nakamura Kusatao

Winter already —
one gravestone looks almost like
a wayside marker   Nakamura Kusatao

Abortion doctor —
sounds of instruments clinking —
yellow leaf-fall days   Ishihara Yatsuka

Isolation cell —
sleeping with one apple on
my prison birthday   Akimoto Fujio

I begin to cut
the Christmas cake, not knowing
anything of Christ   Yamaguchi Hatsume

On this winter night
of the world, I want something
tender, like scrotums   Mori Sumio

12

As if sucking lips,
when I sip nectar from
a peach's white flesh

Uemura Sengyo

Pomegranate seeds —
how many must I eat to
end my loneliness?

Hashimoto Takako

Winter — I am living
surrounded by the houses
of the filthy rich

Hayashi Shō

Into the sea-waves
driving wedges of whiteness —
the drifting seagulls

Katō Kōko

Autumn waterfall —
as if a horse's tail kept
shaking and shaking

Ishizaki Rokufū

Raging top — possessed
utterly by the children's
violent spirits

Ōtake Noriyuki

The new bamboo shoot
making a crack in the earth
listens to the wind

Miyauchi Shuntō

Glimmer of fireflies
through the paper bag — even
more evanescent

Nishio Reiko

In green tree-shadows —
but perhaps it is a trap —
one chair is standing

Mochizuki Tetsudo

The first butterly
makes the sunlight disappear
when it folds its wings

Miyauchi Shuntō

Homecoming — three stars
in winter make a complete
set of shining studs

Kōji Fukunaga

AYAKO HOSOMI

Thunder in springtime —
the thickness of midnight lies
heavy on my chest

Something so distinct
in the very faintness of
the distant thunder

The white peach, just picked —
it seems to be breathing with
its entire body

The air is heavy
on the peach blossom — there are
so many flowers

The grass-burning fires
are spreading — catching now on
the pampas grasses

A snail is clinging
to the mulberry tree in
the wind of autumn

Swallow O swallow
you mud lover O lover
swallow O swallow

In faint morning dark,
a chilliness from the snow
clinging to my belt

The red winter sky
comes to an end, as if all
had come to an end

Single streak of snow
turning to water on
the Golden Temple   Arima Akito

This Golden Temple —
even early summer rain
leaving it untouched   Bashō

Grill mugwort rice cakes
till they are grilled the colour
of Tempyo Era   Arima Akito

Summer daybreak comes
early, deep in the tree's heart,
with the tree's voices   Katō Kōko

Under starry skies
spirits begin drifting —
sorrowing seaweeds   Iida Ryūta

In the autumn breeze
squatting posture of
a sumo referee   Awano Seiho

Spitting out my blood,
my eyes drying up, under
glaring summer heat   Ishihara Yatsuka

Where the atomic
bomb blasted, a child turned to
a shimmer of light   Ishihara Yatsuka

A snail being rocked
on a mulberry tree —
the wind of autumn   Hosomi Ayako

In the petals of
a pink — something of the past
seen even fainter   Matsuzawa Akire

At last, death in action —
a single ant — however far
it tries to go — however far —   Katō Shūson

15

Mounting the stream to
their final death-throes, salmon
set net bells ringing

Awano Seiho

A dragonfly perches
on the edge of a box marked
"This side up"

Awano Seiho

Shaken by sudden sobs,
I dropped the chopsticks for my
seven herbs gruel

Awano Seiho

With my fading sight
my eyes are dazzled even
by one winter rose

Katō Shūson

Through trees now naked
of leaves, the heavens appear
deeper than ever

Katō Kōko

New Year morning breaks
from one rose that is blooming
amid the hoar-frost

Mizuhara Shūōshi

The stridulations
of crickets drilling the rocks —
how quiet it is!

Bashō

This radiant night —
a rising moon the colour
of dried apricot

Mori Sumio

Looking carefully —
shepherd's purse flowering
alongside the fence

Bashō

Through the mountain haze
a woodpecker's hammerings
begin to echo

Sano Ryōta

Upon the snowfield
the eagle has descended
on his own shadow

Yamaguchi Sōdō

16

When he feels lonely
he may start beating his wings —
eagle in a cage   Ishida Hakyō

All through the long night
I was walking round the pond
under bright moonlight   Bashō

When I had finished
cleaning the lamp — cuckoo woods
lay all around me   Shimoda Minoru

Rowing all alone —
cuckoo calling from the woods
to my right and left   Hachiki Ema

Before I could show
my love, the ladybird flew
away from my palm   Akio Kakurai

At last they play our
cherry blossom elegy —
the Kimigayo   Takaya Shōshū

Who could have planted
daffodils upon the grave
of a prostitute?   Tsugawa Kagako

Working on dance steps,
my kimono becomes so
laden with sweat   Han Takehara

Many-layered clothes:
too heavy for my old age,
this dancing costume   Han Takehara

Sweating in autumn,
I forget how old I am,
spend my dance in dance   Han Takehara

HAIKU ECHOES

Two recent items in the French literary press have aroused some haikuesque echoes in me. The first is from *"Libération"* (5 March 1992), a review of François Jullien's philosophic work on Chinese aesthetics, *Eloge de la fadeur*, which might unsatisfactorily be translated as *In Praise of Dullness*: the French word is much more poetic and evocative, and English semi-equivalents like 'insipidity' or 'colourlessness' of 'tastelessness' are too negative. For the Chinese, *fadeur* is a positive quality.

Jullien tells us that the artist Ni Zan (14th C.) painted the same sort of picture all his life: trees along a river bank, a stretch of water, vague hills, an abandoned tea-house. This element of 'sameness' or 'colourless ordinariness' is part of all Chinese thought, art, poetry, and can be said to be present in much Japanese writing. It is also said to be present, unobtrusively, in calligraphy.

In China, the concept is more positive and definite than in the West, to the extent of signifying the opposite of ennui or dullness, and developing the idea of a 'dull existence' as an aesthetic ideal. We are reminded of the polite Chinese curse: 'May you live in stirring times.'

Chinese 'dullness' is a form of almost philosophical acceptance of the ordinary, the insignificant, leading to an appreciation or even reverence for what we in the West may regard as trivial or tasteless or colourless. Thus in a world free from all insistence upon our reactions or our immediate dynamic response to anything that thrusts itself upon our attention, the mind is liberated and able to appreciate the ordinary at its true worth. It is a quietist approach to non-violent attentiveness in which one is alert to the aesthetic values of the understated and the unobtrusive.

Nabakov said that if we look long enough at even the most banal object — the more banal the better — it becomes endowed with interest and charm. The sage seeks to attain this level of detachment in his perception of ordinariness, and thus become disposed to a greater elevation of the mind. The wise man cultivates an awareness of his own platitude and insignificance, and having attained this realization is on the path of wisdom.

The concept of dullness extends, as one might expect, to culinary matters, where the 'discreet quality' of the insipid is able to co-exist with 'the five savours' — acid, bitter, sweet, acrid, salty — whereas strong savours oppose and create division in the elements of a dish. So dullness is primordial harmony, hidden from the negligent daily world, and the secret principle of true aesthetic and spiritual balance. Roland Barthes, on his return from China in 1975, used the word *fadeur* to qualify the general impression that Chinese life had left upon him. It was an acute perception.

The second item was in "*Le Monde*" on the following day, March 6. The headline to an exhibition of photographs by Arnaud Claass at the Galerie Michèle Chamette in Paris ran: "*Eloge de la Banalité.*" (In Praise of the Banal). The article describes how Claass avoids all spectacular, anecdotic and narrative elements in his photographs in favour of presenting objects of a banal ordinariness, inconspicuous in their essential *quidditas*. This theoretician among modern photographers writes in his working notes: "Perhaps obvious things allow us to see that nothing is obvious." And: "I have photographed not so much the banality of things as their halo of feeling." He calls his studies metaphors of eventlessness.

Claass apparently learned the value of the banal in America in the '70's, from long study of the works of Walker Evans, Edward Weston, Lee Friedlander or Ralph Gibson. So he presents us with a pepper, a tree trunk, a shell in a visually meditative way that brings out the 'halo' of hidden life in such ordinary objects. His obsession, he says, is photographing the simple existence of things and showing them in a way that lets the viewer realize he has confidence in such a manner of presentation, without having recourse to large-scale, visually demanding subjects that cry out for our violent reaction to them.

It seems to me that both these items are helpful for our view of what haiku are and how they should be written. They also help to show others who are as it were blind to the ordinary and the dull in our over-emphatic, hyper-emotional modern world that the small and the insignificant have their own modest place among all the clamour of life, and are possessed of their own secret dignity, endurance and presence.

I think a true haiku can express that 'halo' surrounding the ordinary, bring out its secret charm and uniqueness in very few words — the modesty of the means equivalent to the modesty of the subject, which can, when seen in the light of aesthetic meditation and spiritual insight, take on much wider universal meanings and emotions.

Francois Jullien: *Eloge de la Fadeur* Ed. Philippe Picqier, 1922.

Jullien has brought out at the same time *La Propension des Choses*. Collection 'Des Travaux', Seuil.

***

Though people call it
a white peony, it still
has a hint of pink   Takahama Kyoshi

Swaying peonies —
hundreds of them — are just like
boiling hot water   Mori Sumio

Roses collapsing
as if something dreadful is
about to happen   Hashimoto Takako

After our farewell
the scent of the gardenias
still hangs about me   Nakata Yomei

Gardenia blossoms
are just like letters — fading
away so quickly   Nakamura Kusatao

I still remember
on my shoulder the coffin's
weight — sky of fresh leaves   Nakajima Takeo

Poppies flowering —
I cannot do anything —
I am sick again   Matsumoto Takashi

Black underfoot,
mulberries on the road to
the cemetery   Nishijima Bukanan

The futon. Dying —
not enough strength now to kick
back the god of death   Takahama Kyoshi

A fire in the hearth —
a way of life here that I
never knew before   Hoshino Tatsuko

Can't bear even a child
coming close — maybe fatigue
of cold coming on   Nagano Hōsei

Hunters and wild ducks
occupying the same lake —
waiting for daybreak   Tsuda Kiyoko

Don't give up all hope —
cutting down a winter tree
see its bright pink heart   Kasai Teruo

Without the cattle
a plough is just scrap iron:
days getting longer   Hirahata Seitō

On the school blackboard
reminder to pay the fees —
winter vacation   Kamei Itoyū

From the time the sun
comes up, until it goes down —
the blue-green headland   Yamaguchi Seishi

The one black goldfish
appears to me like a bat
flying in water   Yamaguchi Seishi

Looking both high and
low — the right way to admire
tinted foliage   Inahata Teiko

Colour not ready
yet for earth-return — but called
cherry petal dust   Inahata Teiko

Bright just after snow
or even darkened by snow —
this is Tōno country   Inahata Teiko

Shall I stop drinking?
— but what other appetite
should I indulge?   Kaneko Tōta

With his eyes tight closed,
a shepherd is turned towards
the red plum blossoms   Kaneko Tōta

Like the last traces
of snow among the beech trees,
I lie slumbering   Kaneko Tōta

When the cat left home
all that remained in the dark
was the daphne's scent   Kinichi Sawaki

Have the forsythias
at Yotsuyamitsuke
begun blooming yet?   Kinichi Sawaki

All heaven and earth
at the greenest of greenness —
a pheasant runs past   Kinichi Sawaki

Sounding like raindrops
dancing in the fire —
hairy caterpillars   Awano Seiho

Perestroika per
estroika perestroika
crickets getting loud   Awano Seiho

Never again no
never again return into these
deep cicada holes   Awano Seiho

AWANO SIEHO

In our materialistic modern times of industrial and financial rivalries among the great powers, it has become a commonplace in western business circles to label the Japanese as 'economic animals.' Indeed, in a kind of humorous self-defence, they have adopted the cliché themselves. But it should not allow us to forget that this aspect of life in Japan is a minor and possibly temporary trend, and that ideals of beauty and the cultivation of all forms of art reach popular levels unknown in our western society.

For example, in the world of poetry alone — an art now almost extinct as far as the general British public is concerned — it has been estimated recently that there are around 20,000,000 haiku poets in Japan who write haiku regularly, professionally or as a hobby. They belong to an estimated 1,200 haiku organizations, each publishing its own magazine, in which only paid-up members may appear — for each group tries strenuously to ignore all the others. Members frequently travel abroad to seek new images and ideas for their compositions, either of individual haiku or in the form of linked verses created as a communal effort and known as *renku*.

The art of haiku is practised by people from all walks of life, and even industrialists, economists and leading politicians write these brief verses of 17 syllables. Even after falling into disgrace connected with financial scandals, they continue writing haiku. Prisoners on death row write haiku as a form of confessional therapy to prepare themselves for execution often long delayed. Old age pensioners living in old people's homes form haiku groups and go on *ginko* of haiku rambles in the countryside, especially in autumn, to gather poetic impressions: it has been proved scientifically that the writing of haiku keeps the brain active and young, just as the light physical exertion of these open-air rambles keeps the body fit. It has long been noted that haiku poets often live to a grand old age.

Such was the case of the veteran haiku exponent Awano Seiho who recently passed away, still writing, at the ripe age of

93. He was the oldest of the better-known haiku poets who at the beginning of the Showa Era exerted a considerable influence on the art of haiku. He belonged to a group that came to be known as 'the four S's' because their first name (the one haiku poets are usually known by) began with an 'S' — the three others being Yamaguchi Seishi, Mizuhara Shūōshi and Takano Soju.

Modern haiku starts with the 'sketch' form in fairly free style by Masaoka Shiki, who handed down his artistic theories to Takahama Kyoshi, whose literary disciple Awano Seiho became. Generally speaking, the aim of these new poets was to depict the ordinary things and events in daily life in an impressionistic rather than a formal way, deliberately choosing contemporary imagery and using commonplace or even banal words and expressions. A typical example by Seiho from his 1986 collection *Joya* (New Year's Eve) is:

Sucking a persimmon
a seed suddenly popped
into my mouth

which has something of the quality of the Zen experience known as *satori* or spiritual illumination, often brought on by some incongruous happening or association of images.

Seiho wrote simply and directly, without pretentious philosophizing or anguished soul-searchings, though he often used images taken from Buddhism, presented in a characteristic matter-of-fact way. He wrote as the ordinary man in the street writes haiku. Always he adopted a low, humble stance towards the art he devoted his whole life to. It was typical of the modesty of the man that he would accept offers to judge the many haiku contests sponsored by organizations as different as funeral parlours, cake companies, tea merchants — and Japan Air Lines, who have done so much to promote interest in haiku, not only in Japan, but internationally. Another famous haiku poet, Yamaguchi Seison, claimed that Seiho often read the dictionary in order to find inspiration in new, unusual or simply beautiful words which he would then incorporate in a haiku. He is represented in *Gendai*

Haiku (Modern Haiku) and his work often appeared in magazines and newspapers. A series of brief studies of his poems has been appearing during the past year or so in the Nagoya international haiku magazine, *Ko*, edited by the haiku poet Katō Kōko. One of these refers to a haiku trip he made to Shanghai four years ago, in which he writes about the humble rice dumplings eaten during autumn moon-viewing:

> Cramming my mouth with
> getsu-pei, Lake Sei
> remains unruffled

This was composed at the celebrated beauty-spot, the lake in Hang zhou in the People's Republic of China.

For the last fourteen years, the *Asahi Shimbun* newspaper has been printing, right in the middle of its first page, not the latest financial deals and squabbles, but a poetry column of haiku and tanka (the 31-syllable poetic form), something no other newspaper in the world would dare do. And once a week, every Friday, mass circulation newspapers like the *Asahi Shimbun* and *The Yomiuri* print a whole page of haiku received from readers in Japan and all over the world. It was in such an atmosphere favourable to the popular passion for poetry that old poets such as Awano Seiho, and a growing number of younger haiku poets, made their name.

Awano Seiho, born Nara, Feb. 10th 1899. Haiku poet.
Died Nishinomiya, December 22, 1992.

***

26

Green plums — their bottoms
all so beautifully
arranged in order   Murō Saisei

White chysanthemums
gradually embracing
evening shadows   Kubota Mantarō

Treading underfoot
runner vines, the whole mountain's
dews started shaking   Hara Sekitei

A morning glory
shrivelled up, as if desire
had all been satisfied   Hino Sōjō

Apricot blossoms —
the buzzing of bees bringing
Annunciation   Kawabata Bōsha

All the sick patients
stretching out their white hands to
autumn leaf bonfires   Ishida Hakyō

Daybreak in winter —
the sickbeds of six patients
slowly emerging   Ishida Hakyō

Chamber pot making
sounds of a fountain playing —
evening in autumn   Ishida Hakyō

Waiting for the bus
I'm sure spring has come at last
to the boulevard   Ishida Hakyō

I found a lost path
under the moonlight leaking
through white birch tree leaves   Ishibashi Tatsunosuke

My dead friend seemed to
put his hand on my shoulder —
the autumn sun warm   Nakamura Kusatao

Carried away on
the back of a passing horse —
the winter sunshine   Nakamura Kusatao

With his golden eyes
glittering, a sleeping snake
in hibernation   Tamaki Makoto

His eyelids lowered —
Buddha with the broken nose —
deepening winter   Tamaki Makoto

Paper windows all
taken down for cleaning leave
just temple pillars   Nomura Toshirō

First cold — one thousand
pickled turnip slices just
start getting sticky   Nomura Toshirō

Something with rising
steam has just been carried in —
a midnight supper   Nomura Toshirō

With a basket of
seven spring herbs — she seems to
become much taller   Ishihara Yatsuka

When winter has come
there appear, dancing in the
empty air, shadows   Ishihara Yatsuka

Whirling wintry winds
drilling down the government
office district streets   Ishihara Yatsuka

In cherry blossom
season, the clouds are always
a nondescript grey   Katsura Nobuko

A glasshouse flower
keeps company with bigfaced
aquarium fish   Katsura Nobuko

Distant fireworks
in the company of this
mild-mannered person   Katsura Nobuko

With just one finger
tip, the whole pond, covered in
thin ice, can be moved   Gotō Hinao

Clouds coming and clouds
departing — golden yellow
flowers of the spring   Gotō Hinao

I wish that heaven
could also be paradise
even for the ants   Gotō Hinao

Beautiful young boys
still in the flower of spring
sixty years later   Nagata Kōi

A beautiful boy —
easy come, but easy go —
thin ice in springtime   Nagata Kōi

The mating of snails —
I wonder, does their meat screw
deep into the other's?   Nagata Kōi

29

BASHŌ: *JOURNAUX DE VOYAGE*

Translated by René Sieffert. Publications Orientalistes de France

123 pp. FF 90.00 ISBN 9 782716 902670

This spring marks the three hundredth anniversary of Matsuo Bashō's best known sequence of prose and poetry, *Oku no hosomichi* (The Narrow Road to the Deep North). This interesting form of journal, *haïbun*, so sadly lacking in British literature, proves, as his gifted translator points out, that Bashō was a fine prose writer as well as a great poet.

Sieffert, celebrated for his translations of a large body of classical Japanese literature, including what is so far the most beautiful version of *The Tale of Genji*, provides a concise introduction to *haïbun* and the evolution of haiku from the earliest collection of *waka*, the *Kokin-waka-shû* compiled in 905 by imperial command. Book XIX contains some 31-syllable *tanka* whose expression is freer than the more severe tone of the *waka*, with its strict vocabulary and official poetic rules. *Haikai* and haiku sequences known as *renga* did not however become accepted until the 17th century, despite the scorn of the purists, and Bashō was the first great master of the 17-syllable form.

The travel diaries here presented include all the famous ones to be found in the Penguin edition, in some ways unsatisfactory, translated and introduced by Professor Nobuyuki Yuasa, together with the later Saga journal which, unlike the other diaries, is dated day by day, and therefore is a precious document of the poet's daily life, showing the extraordinary intellectual and poetic ferment of which he was the centre when he stayed at the "house of the falling persimmons", now a celebrated tourist spot on the plain of Saga, north-west of Kyoto. Sieffert also adds what is not strictly speaking a journal, the brief *Notes from the Genjuû-an Hermitage* overlooking Lake Biwa, where Bashō passed the summer of 1690. These notes constitute a kind of poetic or even philosopic testament, fresh and appealing in this translation. They seem to give the true portrait of this totally unpedantic and un-doctrinaire genius, always so closely attached to the small things of nature, and to the wider landscapes of Japan:

> I have simply become a man of the mountains, carefree,
> ...sitting on a deserted slope to catch my fleas.

The beauty of Bashō's prose, so well conveyed by Sieffert's elegant French style, can best be seen in his descriptions of landscape in the "far north" of Sendai, Shiogama, Matsushima, Kinkazan and Hiraizumi in *Oku no hosomichi*. Travel in those days was slow and uncomfortable, but though he was often weary and sick with what seems to have been either severe asthma or a weak heart, his poetic spirit never fails him, so that at the Shirakawa barrier, then considered the gateway to the unknown, he could write: "Here at last I can feel within me the soul of a traveller."

He who always reminded his disciples that "haiku come from the heart" scatters his travel diaries with poems that have become the literary heritage of every Japanese. Some of Sieffert's versions seem to me a little stiff, containing as they do certain archaic inversions that nevertheless give us a reminder of the original word-order:

> *Ah le silence*
> *et vrille et vrille le roc*
> *le cri des cigales*

but not, as can be seen, the original syllabic count, which is preserved in my own translation of this popular haiku:

> Song of cicadas —
> stridulations drill the rocks —
> how quiet it is

***

URAI FUMIE

Treading frost needles
I feel something is running
underneath my soles

A child is sketching,
making the cosmos flowers
so big, so thick

Water dripping from
the eaves, irradiating
February light

On my palm, I feel
the bunch of grapes weighing with
its own heaviness

Gathering the wind
pure green as green can be, in
picked tea-leaf baskets

Regret fall's leaving —
watch the sea till my body
becomes transparent

A chilly darkness
within the depths of her womb —
an unlighted kiln

The white peony
collapsed — making the ground look
all that much darker

Watching the wind on
the surface of the water —
a dragonfly's eyes

A new bride buying
bunch of celery in May —
making a fresh start

Born out of a mist
of crimson — the radiance of
first cherry blossom

A thin moon hanging
upon the ancient pine tree —
a house on the bay

Underneath the moon
a village — heaven and earth,
too, start from the sea

***

Dropping behind in
May Day parade, carrying
sleepy child on back   Satō Kibō

On the salt pot, SALT
in dead mother's handwriting
on this Mother's Day   Kawamoto Keishi

Horse race festival —
one horse keeps playing around,
just can't get started   Takahama Kyoshi

I'm listening to
such a tragic story — while
licking an ice cream   Iwasaki Fukuko

The cry of a toad —
ashes of death are falling
to the earth at night   Ishihara Yatsuka

A lizard's tail falls
off, and goes on dancing all
alone, ecstatic   Katō Shūson

A snake slithered off;
the eyes that flashed at me still
linger in the grass   Takahama Kyoshi

33

After catching sight
of a snake, its glaring eyes
haunt me all the time

Nozawa Setsuko

They are measuring
the full length of the serpent
they have done to death

Genshi Kōhei

A young viper's head
smashed to pieces, but his tail
still whips angrily

Saitō Sanki

I never knew love
for a child: so I scatter
food for my goldfish

Katsura Nobuko

While handling his yacht,
a youth already learning
a cigarette's taste

Hasegawa Rōrōshi

A child in a dream
suntanned and always smiling
makes its mother cry

Fukuda Jintō

All these many years
struggling to earn money — and
this damned athlete's foot

Niikura Yafū

Peonies — a hundred,
two hundred, three hundred, but
with only one gate

Awano Seiho

Just like playing trumps —
the roses in the vase all
fall on each other

Watanabe Suiha

The breath of roses —
listening to it as to
a quickening child

Nishijima Bakunan

The petals falling
smash down upon the petals
of other roses

Shinohara Bon

After mother's death
most of the lane is covered
by summer grasses   Enomoto Fuyuichirō

On the waggons of
goods trains, the graffiti start
running: fume of grass   Genshi Kōmei

Lightning flash exposing
feet and hands I secretly
gave to a lover   Katsura Nobuko

Roaring winter waves
of the ocean, that one day
will scatter my bones   Katsura Nobuko

My balls hanging down
in limitless contentment —
drinking cold sake   Fujita Shōshi

Eclipse of the sun —
in the darkness, peonies
drink life to the full   Ayako Hosomi

A red moth came out
dancing in broad daylight — war-end
anniversary   Fujita Shōshi

A new calendar —
unknown days, weeks and months now
look so beautiful   Yoshiya Nobuko

Spinning tops of fire —
red camellias float away
upon the current   Nomiyama Asuka

The white peony,
released from the wind, returns
to its former shape   Hoshino Tsunehiko

Standing with back to
the dark — policeman's view
of cherry blossoms   Hoshino Tsunehiko

MY THEME IS "GRASS"

Grass is a universal poetic image. Psalm 103 in the Bible tells us:

> As for man, his days are as grass: as flower of the field he flourisheth. For the wind passeth over it, and it is gone...

The image of grass is often associated with death, and with the aftermath of war. Indeed, the original meaning of the word "aftermath" comes from grass that has been mowed, or that is growing again after being mowed. The Scots poet Thomas Campbell wrote in his great anti-war poem "Hohenlinden":

> Few, few shall part, where many meet!
> The snow shall be their winding sheet,
> And every turf beneath their feet
>   Shall be a soldier's sepulchre.

Here the word "turf" suggests grass.

Wordsworth, in his poem "Yarrow Revisited" tells us:

> That life is but a tale of morning grass
> Withered at eve.

The great American poet Walt Whitman called his book of poems *Leaves of Grass* and in one of those poems, "Song of Myself", he says:

> I believe that a leaf of grass is no less than the journey-
>   [work of the stars...

Another great American poet, Carl Sandburg, wrote a poem whose title is "Grass":

> Pile high the bodies at Austerlitz and Waterloo,
> Shovel them under and let me work —
> I am the grass; I cover all.

That image of dead soldiers' bodies killed in a senseless war is particularly topical for us today, when we see such images constantly on our TV screens. It reminds me of Bashō's haiku: *Natsu-kusa ya/ tsuwa-mon-domo ga/ yume no ato*, which I have translated as:

> All that remains of
> those brave warriors' dreamings —
> these summer grasses.

Japanese poetry is also full of images of grass — summer grasses, the fume of summer grass, grass growing high and so on: *muzanyana/ kabutono shita no/ kirigirisu* by Bashō does not contain the word "grass" but but suggests it in the word "grasshoppers" and continues the universal image of the folly of war:

> What pathetic sounds —
> grasshoppers chirping under
> broken war-helmets.

War is usually the result of the stupidity of incompetent politicians; as Jonathan Swift declared in a famous passage from *Gulliver's Travels*, a man who can make corn and grass grow is better than any politician:

> He gave it of his opinion, that whoever could make two
> ears of corn or two blades of grass to grow upon a spot of
> ground where only one grew before, would deserve better
> of mankind, and do more essential service to his country
> than the whole race of politicians put together.

Such is the universal importance of the image of grass in poetry, in life, in death.

***

A wasp in winter
can find no place to die, so
goes crawling around

Murakami Kijō

A fly in winter
crawling around — if he finds
a knife, he'll lick it

Saitō Sanki

Pulling withered vines —
it looks like someone pulling
back hair from behind

Nagaki Kikuno

Women lamenting —
turning to only one tree
in the winter wood

Mitani Akira

I never forget
my father — on his dead face
a fly alighting

Enomoto Toichirō

I hate all creatures —
even at midnight, I keep
hitting at the flies

Mitani Akira

Maggots are hatching
all over the rotting flesh —
no eyes, no nose left

Nakatome Sotoya

Suddenly, I saw
my own dead body starting
to crawl with maggots

Nomiyama Asuka

Dead butterfly's wings
still working, trying to
take off on the wind

Tamaki Makoto

Old widows' home
living with bedbugs only
and the love of Christ

Fujimori Shin

How deep the pitch dark
of the night in which I fling
a gold bug away

Takahama Kyoshi

Into the darkness
from which it came, throwing back
a gold bug beetle   Shinohara Bon

Here you are living
the life of a greenbottle fly — and
you say such a thing!   Katō Shūson

Caught between index
and thumb, the silverfish turned
to my fingerprint   Ōishi Sekibutsu

Mountain ant aflame
with sunset at sea, climbing
up a pine tree trunk   Hashimoto Yoshinori

Among the new leaves'
myriad green, my child's first
teeth start coming out   Nakamura Kusatao

I let a young girl
feel the touch of cold iron
on a hunting gun   Kasuma Tokihiko

The shining barrel
of his rifle — the eyes of
a hunter passing   Washitani Nanako

The moon in winter
entangled in the halyards
of a sailing ship   Takahama Kyoshi

Waiting for the spring —
a stick is left standing in
a sickroom corner   Ishida Hakyō

The first calendar —
turning the days and months, time
starts flowing away   Igarashi Bansui

The first calendar —
among the days, one when I
become an uncle   Umemura Kōbun

39

Some of them singing
to their heart's content — clear-toned
evening cicadas   Kaneko Tōta

I keep on, keep on —
but can't get out from under
this giant rainbow   Usaki Fuyuo

Mountain grass burning —
fire traces at night lie side
by side with the stars   Maruyama Bōsui

Spring melancholy —
yet I am dimly aware
of a certain hunger   Nomura Toshirō

Like a beast lying
soiled and stained along the ground —
the last of the snow   Ōhashi Ōhashi

During the pruning
the severed twigs keep falling
out of the blue sky   Yuasa Katsuji

April Fool — even
when I'm sick, and don't eat much,
I just can't lose weight   Katō Chiyoka

I swung on my swing
close to my father — then swung
back to my mother   Hashimoto Takako

***

YAMAGUCHI SEISHI

Blossoming plum boughs
arranged with one branch pressed
hard against a wall

Beautiful — seven
days of springitme beginning
over and over

Water already
stained with blood — they still go on
cleaning yellowtails

Leaving the castle,
one cherry blossom petal
still drifting on air

A beautiful girl —
fingering the brim of her
rice-planting sedge hat

Looking into a
jar of pickled plums as if
into the abyss

Ten trillion miles of
paradise permeating
all the afterglow

The smallest creatures —
even silverfish — increase
and flee together

Voices of wild geese
so closely intermingled
as if wing to wing

Robbed of their nestlings
the parent sparrows flying
around and around

Folded are the screens
that during the encampment
enclosed so many

Out on the ocean
lights of an unknown village —
village of squid boats

Here all of Japan
comes to pay its first respects at
the shrine of this New Year

My swimming pants off
a whiteness still unchanged since
the day I was born

Wailing of the wind
as it recites again and then again
again its old tale

Blowing out to sea,
winter winds can find no place
to come back home to

Bonfire at its height
the kanji "Great" is written
with a loaded brush

***

SEISHI (CHIKAHIKO) YAMAGUCHI

When he was born, his parents gave him the name of Chikahiko. But like most haiku poets, he adopted a more dignified pen-name, Seishi. He was the first child of Yamaguchi Shinsuke and Mineko. As was the case with many Japanese writers and artists, he had a very disturbed childhood and youth. At the normal age of seven he entered Kinrin Elementary School in Kyoto, but the next year he was sent away from home to live with his maternal grandfather in Tokyo. So he had to transfer to the local elementary school. But two years later, in 1911, his grandfather became general manager of a newspaper in far-off Sakhalin, the "Karafuto Nichinichi Shimbun" and took the arduous voyage to that lonely colonial outpost of Japan seized by Japanese forces at the end of the Russo-Japanese War. Being sent to Karafuto on the island of Sakhalin, far to the north of northernmost Japan, was in those days like being sent to Siberia, but in July of 1912 Chikahiko sailed there to join his grandfather. His mother Mineko had committed suicide in June, 1911, an event that was to haunt the poet all his life.

On arrival in Karafuto, Chikahiko again had to enter a new school, the Toyohara Elementary School. The 1914 school year began with his transference to Ōdamari Middle School, and it was here, at the age of thirteen, that his vocation as a haiku poet may be said to have begun. His Japanese language teacher, Nagai Teppei, began instructing him in the composition of traditional haiku, and the boy soon developed a veritable passion for the form.

In 1917 he left Karafuto and returned to Kyoto, where he attended the Kyoto First Middle School, and in 1919 he entered the liberal arts department of the Third High School.

In October 1920 he experienced his first introduction to the real life of the haiku world when he took part in the Kyoto Imperial University and the Third High School Haiku Conference. He started to receive guidance in his writing from notable haiku poets like Sōjō Hino and Noboru Suzuka. He submitted the first haiku to the famous haiku magazine "Hotogisu" and signalled his new status as a poet by writing his name with different characters for Chikahiko.

In March 1922, he had his first encounter with one of the great modern exponents of the art of haiku, Kyoshi Takahama, who read the new characters in Yamaguchi's name and pronounced it Seishi. The poet's haiku name was finally recognized. The following month, he met another celebrated haiku poet, Shūōshi Mizuhara. April is the official beginning of the academic year in Japan, and Yamaguchi met Shūōshi when he moved to Tokyo to enter the law department of the Imperial University. At once, along with like-minded haiku poets like Shūōshi, Fūsei Tomiyasu and others, Yamaguchi began the revival of the University of Tokyo Haiku Conference. It was the start of a life devoted to the propagation of haiku.

It was also to be a life of internal disagreements with various haiku societies, and changes in Yamaguchi's own conception of what haiku should be. After graduating, he started work in April, 1926 at the main office of the Sumitomo Bank.

In 1928 his beloved grandfather died. His sorrow was alleviated by marriage to another haiku poet, Umeko Asai, whose pen name was Hatsujo, herself the daughter of a *haïjin*. They set up house in Osaka, where Seishi's haiku reputation continued to grow, and he was elected to the editorial board of "Hototogisu" — the first of several such positions he was to hold.

He published his first book of haiku, *Tōkō* (Frozen Harbour) in May 1932. But he gradually became dissatisfied with the "Hotogisu" group's strict adherence to the objective description of nature, and in 1935, after publishing his second book of haiku, *Kōki* (Yellow Flag), he joined the "Ashibi" haiku group, directed by Shūōshi. His third book, *Enchū* (Summer Noon) was published by a major firm, Sanseidō, in 1938.

During the war years, Seishi continued writing, and Sanseidō published his fourth book *Shichiyō* (Seven Days of the Week) in 1942. In June 1945, his house in Osaka was destroyed by a bombing raid, and his father died.

Seishi went on creating new poems and introducing new elements into the formal haiku. Even his first collection had been ground-breaking, for Kyoshi Takehama had written of it: "In his haiku the poet moves into areas unheard-of in the past... His criticism, too, has a precision that gives evidence of a very individual viewpoint in the present haiku world." Seishi sought subjects for haiku not just in nature but also in the works of man:

44

> In the summer grass
> wheels of a locomotive
> coming to a stop.

Here, though the main image is a modern industrial one, Seishi still preserves the hallowed use of a "season word", *natsukusa* or "summer grass." This poem was composed in 1933, and though to us its modernism does not seem at all unusual, at that time it created a sensation in the haiku world. He went on to write about urban life, dockyards, steamships, skating rinks, hotels, dance halls, elevators, whaling ships, swimming pools and even about Christmas — the first step towards incorporation into haiku of images associated with western traditions, like Saint Valentine's Day, Guy Fawkes Day, and with symbols of foreign travel like the Tower of London and the Champs Elysées.

In all, Seishi published seventeen books of haiku, and hundreds of his poems have been carved in stone all over Japan. He received many awards: the Japan Academy Award (1987), the "Asahi" Newspaper Award (1989) and the National Award for Cultural Merit (1992). He started his own haiku magazine, *Tenrō* (Sirius) in 1948, and from 1957 almost to the time of his death was the chief selector of haiku sent in to the "Asahi" newspaper's weekly page of poems by haiku poets all over Japan, and by Japanese and foreign haiku poets from abroad.

The Essence of Modern Haiku, a collection of three hundred of his poems in Japanese, *romaji* and English translation was published in Atlanta, Georgia by Mangajin Inc. in 1993, and introduced him to a very wide audience of foreign haiku enthusiasts.

With the death of Seishi Yamaguchi, we mourn the passing of the last of that great quartet of Tokyo University haiku innovators who, because their pen-names all began with "S" were always popularly known as "The Four S's" — Seiho Awano, Suju Takano and Shūōshi Mizuhara were the other three.

***

45

Temples in autumn
only start brightening up
just at someone's death — Arima Akito

A tree like a hand
sticking up from the waters
of a dam in autumn — Tanino Yoshi

Somewhere round the stone
Buddha, there are eggs of snakes
slowly ripening — Ishida Hakyō

As it was lifting
its head, I first realized
snakes have a shadow — Tamaki Makoto

Rusting in grasses
forgotten coiled iron chain —
serpent in autumn — Tamaki Makoto

The butterfly's wings
shimmering even brighter
than the sky above — Yamaguchi Seishi

Cupping both my hands,
I scoop up a cricket that
dropped into my hearth — Iida Dakotsu

Sleeping all alone,
I share the same darkness with
the household cricket — Katsura Nobuko

The caged grasshopper —
unable to bear its song
at night, I free it — Kanao Umenomon

When I walk, the squeak
of my artificial leg —
a grashopper's chirp — Amano Bakushūshi

Beneath the pillow
where my grey hairs are pulled out,
a cricket chirping — Bashō

A winter rose's
single flower is being
jostled by the wind   Takahama Kyoshi

Nearer to heaven
than the lark — rest at the top
of the mountain pass   Bashō

These longer days seem
not enough for the lark, who
still keeps on singing   Bashō

God hung this rainbow,
and in the goodness of time
God will take it down   Yamaguchi Seishi

Breasting a path through
red dragonflies, a farmer
is making his way   Saitō Sanki

On running water
chasing his own reflection
goes the dragonfly   Kagano Chiyojo

Pausing in my walk
I see all around me more
and more dragonflies   Nakamura Teijô

A distant mountain
reflected in the eyeballs
of a dragonfly   Issa

Dragonfly flying —
distant mountain colours through
his transparent wings   Yamaguchi Seison

Every time I look
a dragonfly perches on top
of that bamboo pole   Shiki

A man, becoming
old, starts loving other men —
arrowroot flower   Nagata Kōi

47

ROBERT BRESSON

A famous French film-maker's haikuesque sensiblity

The work of the film director Robert Bresson is distinguished by extreme care for the details of setting, characterization, sound and silence. He detests the "star system" and prefers to use non-professional actors whom he calls *modèles*. His aim is to allow these men and women to reveal their innermost humanity in a strictly-controlled yet natural manner.

Bresson (b. 1901) who trained as a painter before turning to the cinema (which he prefers to call cinématographe) creates works of the utmost refinement in their visual honesty, emotional subtlety and intellectual rigour. In his long life, he has completed only 14 films, but they are all of exceptional quality, and are among the rare cinematographic works that one can enjoy time and time again, always discovering something new at each viewing.

Robert Bresson has published a fascinating collection of notes and aphorisms, *Notes sur le cinématographe*, (Gallimard 1975) with a preface by one of his admirers, the novelist J.M.G. Le Clézio, a writer with some of the same passion of perfection in style and composition as this master of the art of cinematography. Among these apparently casual jottings made during his work during a quarter of a century (1950-1975), I found several examples that at once reminded me of the art of haiku. This is not really surprising, when one considers how deeply Bresson has been influenced by another perfectionist in the cinema, Yasujiro Ozu.

There are some notes covering film-making in general which can be applied to the making of haiku:

A collection of fine images can become detestable.
Capturing instants. Spontaneity, freshness.
An image of the expected kind (cliché) can never be correct,
even though it may seem to be.
Do not go running after poetry. Let it appear of its own
accord between the lines.

These are thoughts which can be applied to the creation of

haiku. One of Bresson's approaches to his art is to avoid over-intellectualization. On the very last page of his book, he writes: "...let me be removed far from intelligence, which complicates everything." A similar attitude is needed in order to catch the flashing moment of a good haiku, which cannot be produced simply by taking thought: as St Matthew says: "Which of you by taking thought can add one cubit to his stature?" (6:27). Instinct, flair and often happy accident (uncontrolled by reason) are basic elements in both film and haiku. The unexpected can be encouraged. Bresson often quotes painters and writers on this theme, as in the revealing remark Renoir made to Matisse:

> I often paint bunches of flowers from the side I had not intended to depict.

Economy of means is something that has to be at the root of all style in haiku as in good film-making:

> He who can make do with less is able to make use of more. He who makes use of more cannot necessarily make do with less.

This seems to me to illustrate admirably the difference between Japanese and English/European stances towards poetic descriptions of nature. I have recently been writing a series of essays comparing English and Japanese themes, choosing first of all some of the most common images in haiku — butterfly, cuckoo, the seasons, moon and stars, insects and so on. I found that while the Japanese view of the subject is generally compressed and precise and to the point, English poems are too diffuse in their imagery, so that an English poet writing about a woodpecker (as Andrew Marvell does in "Upon Appleton House") introduces a host of associated pictures and ideas, and thus the bird itself is lost in all the tapestry-like decoration. Of course, Marvell was writing a long poem, in which he could allow himself far more liberty of expression than a haiku poet. But in the end, it is the haiku poet's vision of the elusive woodpecker that remains most clearly in the memory of the reader:

> Woodpecker pecking —
> hastening the fall of leaves
> from pasturage trees.   (Mizuhara Shūōshi)

On the other hand, Marvell's poem has the qualities of sustained musical and rhythmical expression impossible to achieve in short forms of verse, both in Japanese and English. But in both cases, it could be said that the poet might have been following Bresson's advice: "Poet, forget you are making a poem..." He later says that in order to demonstrate, for example, that a certain husband is ugly, one does not have to show a multitude of ugly husbands, only one. An English poem about a flower or a season will nearly always produce a multitude of extraneous images and comparisons. Quite often English (and European) poets write poems about *all* the seasons, or about a whole bouquet of flowers that bloom at different times of the year — something unimaginable, and undesirable, in haiku.

But again Bresson reminds us of haiku technique when he tells us;

Bring together things that have never before been brought together, and did not seem predestined to be.

That is the theory of "juxtaposition" enunciated by Shiki and his followers, and still followed by contemprary haiku poets. Incidentally, it lies at the heart of all effective surrealist imagery, too.

Quoting again from an artist, Corot, Bresson gives us this thought:

You must not speak, you must wait.

Which reminds me of Picasso's famous dictum: "I do not seek, I *find*". Bresson often refers to the necessity for "attention" or "attentiveness" to images, sounds, silences, so that one shows *discernment* and *precision* in one's perceptions of the world. But is is through the ear, rather than the eye, that one should apprehend human existence:

Our eyes, when they become too fixed in thought, are too intelligent...The eye is usually too superficial, the ear is profound and inventive. The sound of a train whistle can evoke an entire railway station.

The artist has to interpret the invisible as well as the visible world: one of Bresson's aphorisms on this subject fell almost naturally into haiku form:

> Invisible wind
> translated by the water
> sculpted in passing.

And he goes on to say:

> Allow things to appear which without your help would perhaps never be seen.

That is exactly what a good haiku poet does: he reveals the ordinary world that most people pass by without a second glance. But the haiku poet's first glance is the only one he needs: there are no second glances in haiku creation. That is the secret of inspiration, both in the cinema and in poetry:

> When you do not know what you are doing, and when what you do is your very best, that is inspiration.

Bresson describes a sensation familiar to all haiku poets trying to catch the fleeting second on the wing:

> Directing a film. Anxiety not to allow anything to be lost when it has been revealed to me even in the briefest glimpse.

And:

> Do not consciously make beautiful or make ugly. Do not distort the true nature of things... It is the purity of form that is most striking in art.

And:

> The most ordinary word, set in its proper place, all at once takes on a special radiance. It is with that radiance that your images should shine.

All that is good advice for the haiku poet, whether a beginner or a professional. I wish all haiku poets could see, and see again, the superb cinematography of Robert Bresson: all his work breathes haiku feeling, haiku restraint, haiku simplicity.

NOTE: An English translation of Robert Bresson's book was issued by Quartet Books (1986). There are also translations into Japanese (Chikuma Shobo, 1987), German (Hanser, 1978) and Dutch (Sun, 1982).

ARIMA AKITO

A street musician
collecting coins in his hat —
and the falling leaves

Winter coming to
an end now with the quiet
death of the tortoise

An autumn day ends
like the shutting of a drawer
in the chiffonier

Rain long awaited —
only enough to dampen
goddess statues' breasts

A swarming of black
ants — the Holy Bible in
ancient Greek letters

My wife tells me that
her foetus has just the weight
now of a white peach

A bird suddenly
starts uttering human speech —
clothes-changing season

Sit watching wild ducks
migrating — clasping knees as
in urn burials

One man digging deep
graves in winter, and singing
softly to himself

Looking through the light
in lands of the midnight sun —
drinking black beer

Autumn festival —
baking the harvest cakes to
a golden colour

Cherry blossom chill —
wiping a mirror until
it reflects the past

***

SHŪSON KATŌ

Japanese poets usually adopt a pen-name, and when they become famous they are often referred to not by their family name, but by the name they have chosen. Shūson Katō was born Takeo Katō, but this revered and deeply-loved figure of the haiku world is always referred to as Shūson.

His father worked for the railway, and this meant that the Katō family was always changing house as its head was promoted to other posts. They were in Tokyo when their first son, who was to become one of Japan's most celebrated modern haiku poets, was born 26 May, 1905. The parents became converted to Christianity, and when the father was station-master at Ichinoseki in Iwate-ken their son was baptized at the age of thirteen.

Takeo Katō began working as an assistant teacher at Kasukabe Chuo-gakko (Junior High School). Kasukabe is a small town renowned throughout Japan for its centuries-old wisteria vine which has a trunk measuring about nine metres at its base: it is a government protected plant whose flowers reach a length of two metres in mid-May, the season of the poet's birth, when his haiku are recited beneath the blossoms.

But at that time, when he was only sixteen or so, Takeo despised haiku, for he was interested in the rather loftier 31-syllable form, the *tanka*. However, while he was teaching at the school, the local hospital was visited twice a month by a doctor who was also a famed haiku poet. This was Shūōshi Mizuhara. The haiku enthusiasts among the school teachers had admired the work of Kijō Murakami, whose subjects were often weak, helpless creatures arousing pathos and affection in the beholder, as in his most famous verse: "Winter wasp/ no place to die/ so he keeps crawling around." (It is of course impossible to do justice to the tonal beauty of the Japanese words in English translation). Katō and his colleagues at the school approached Mizuhara, who encouraged their writing, and Katō, falling under the older poet's spell, became his life-long disciple, while Mizuhara helped him financially and in other ways: for example, he introduced him to the haiku magazine "Ashibi" whose poets were noted for their delicacy of tone and beauty of rhythmic effects. Katō soon became recognized as a *haïjin* (haiku poet) of exceptional talent, and after only one year of haiku-making won the magazine's second prize.

Shūson (as we should now call him) had married in 1929, and had three children. With Shūōshi's generous help, he entered Tokyo Bunrika Daigaku (the present ultra-modern Tsukuba University) as a freshman student of Japanese literature. In 1939, at the age of 34, again with Shūōshi's encouragement, he published his first collection of haiku, *Kanrai* (Winter Thunder), and in the next year, with the success of his first book, he started his own haiku magazine which bore the same name as his collection, *Kanrai*, and in it he was to print the early work of some of the most admired contemporary haiku poets like Kaneko Tōta and Ando Tsugio. Shūson also became well-known for his scholarly and poetic appreciations of the great classic *haïjin*, notably Matsuo Bashō.

In 1957, Kadokawa Shoten issued a first collected edition of Shūson's works. But the poet fell ill in 1960 and underwent chest operations, presumably for tuberculosis. Yet he continued writing haiku. As he said: "Without my haiku I am nothing. It is only haiku I live for, and only haiku that keep me alive." His faith in the healing power of poetry was such that he gradually recovered. It was in the '60's that Shūson became identified in the popular mind as a poet who wrote in order to explore "how human beings should live."

From 1970, he was engaged by the "Asahi" newspaper to be one of the judges of the submissions for the weekly haiku page, which every week attracted thousands of entries from all over Japan. Today, it is a splendid and heartening sight to see a full page of a modern newspaper devoted not to scandals and politics and money-grubbing but to the noble art of haiku. Shūson also won many prizes for his work, including the Japan Art Academy Prize and the Asahi Prize for Poetry. His life's work was crowned by the publication of his Complete Collected Works by Kōdansha (1980-82).

In April 1993, he fell sick, but again recovered and started the arduous task of choosing the weekly poems for the "Asahi." Alas, on 20 June he lost consciousness: the 11 July issue of the "Asahi" poetry page was his last. It was said that even while he lay unconscious he was moving his fingers in the typical syllable-counting fashion of every haiku poet, bending his fingers inwards towards the palm, then releasing them again one by one. His hands appeared to be shuffling the thousands of postcards that arrived in the "Asahi" offices every week bearing haiku from known and unknown poets, from all over Japan and all over the world.

The even more venerable haiku master, Seishi Yamaguchi, who still chooses poems for the "Asahi" page, even at the ripe age of 91, paid tribute to his fellow poet and newspaper colleague in the pages of the newspaper, regretting that his "junior" (by three years) had died before him. Just before dying, haiku poets usually compose a "death haiku" reverently written down by disciples. There has so far been no announcement of such a poem in the press, but there is one well-known haiku by Shūson, carefully using the "season word" *frost*, which may take its place here for the moment:

> Six feet of soil in
> the frost of earth becomes room
> enough for the dead.

Shūson Katō, haiku poet and scholar, born 26 May 1905, in Tokyo. Died of heart failure 3 July, 1993, in Tokyo. Funeral on 19 July from 1 o'clock at Tokyo Setagaya Joshinji Temple.

***

KATŌ KŌKO

A first bird singing —
the pine tree's gnarled trunk begins
swelling in the sun

Snow-melted waters
running where one thousand stone
Buddhas are standing

Chin resting upon
the handle of a hoe in
the green of the fields

In the flower storm
realizing I was lost
for words completely

Blue-green world of trees
holding enshrined within it
a golden Buddha

Cutting peonies —
the secateurs are all wet
with daybreak dews

Cormorant cressets —
hundreds of scarlet letters
trickling from the fires

Wrapping my hands round
this tea-cup's old yellow glaze —
September going

Like shadow pictures
at the bottom of the sea —
walking in night fog

The voice of the heart
expressing itself only
in panting white breath

MATSUO BASHŌ : SOME HAIKU

Translations and commentaries by James Kirkup

Listening to them
it's hard to beleive they'll soon
die — the cicadas.

One of the advantages of writing English haiku in three lines instead of in one is that we can use English line-ending effects. In English poetry, the ends and beginnings of lines are very sensitive, and words placed in these positions can acquire a special resonance.

In this famous haiku, the placing of "soon" creates a light pause, and almost a feeling of slight suspense before the important word "die", whose isolation at the start of the next line adds to its force.

After "die", a longer pause, using a dash, introduces, right at the last moment, with a certain dramatic surprise, the subject of the poem: "the cicadas." The dash is a useful element in English poetry for the purposes of pace and suspense.

***

The full moon shining —
all night long I've been walking
round and round the pond.

In translation, and also of course in original English poems, punctuation is very effective when carefully used. Punctuation is the musical notation of poetry, and can be used in many subtle ways to indicate speed, tone, rhythm and pauses of varying lengths. In translating haiku, the dash helps to produce impressionistic effects, to accent contrasting images, to both separate and combine apparently conflicting words and ideas.

Here the use of the dash after "shining" helps to prolong that word, and also to emphasize the power of the moonlight. As "shining" is a present participle, it suggests something continuous.

Repetition is another favourite English poetic device. "Round and round" suggests continuity as well as repetition of movement, as does the present participle "walking". Bashō spent all night walking and walking round Hirosawa no ike. Perhaps the strong moonlight stopped him from sleeping after he had spent some hours viewing the full moon. In a play of meanings, "round" also makes us think of the image of the full moon.

We can associate this full moon haiku with another by Bashō that presents quite a different picture, though the moon still remains strong:

> *Sometimes passing clouds*
> *bring us relief from watching*
> *the full moon too long.*

***

> *Upon a dead branch*
> *a crow comes and perches —*
> *evening in autumn.*

Here also the dash after "perches" suggests the sudden pause after the bird alights on the withered branch. By using the form "comes and perches" the actual movemennt is expressed more vividly: we see the crow "coming" before he "perches." The preposition "upon", rather than just "on" also gives a sense of both motion and rest.

Sometimes we can use a dash very effectively at the beginning of a line, or in the middle of a line, like a caesura. But in this haiku, the dash must come at the end of the second line, creating that pregnant pause that fills the third line with such great tranquillity. It is not necessary to make a complete sentence: the three simple words express everything, just as our eye completes spaces left empty by an artist in a painting.

***

> *The bee leaves the heart*
> *of the peony flower*
> *— so reluctantly!*

The dash here could also be at the end of the second line, but it creates an added surprise when placed at the beginning of the last line. I always try to use exclamation marks sparingly, unlike some translators who try to make up for inadequacy of their techniques by putting exclamation marks all over the place, thus robbing them of their true value and tiring the reader's eye. But here I feel my exclamation mark is justified.

The bee is almost drugged by the sweetness at the heart of the peony's rich stamens. Perhaps it is also loaded with pollen and honey and finds it physically difficult to extract itself from the flower. So the dash and the exclamation mark suggest both the bee's pleasure and it struggle to release itself from it, however unwillingly. There is a busy pause, in which we can feel and almost hear the bee at work before it has to leave — "so reluctantly." This haiku reminds me of the famous line in Shakespeare's *Romeo and Juliet*: "Parting is such sweet sorrow..." (Act II, Scene ii).

Insects, however humble, form an important part of the imagery in the work of Bashō and other haiku poets like Issa and Buson. They seem to arouse the fresh spirit of childhood in the poets, as in this haiku by Bashō:

> *Wake up, wake up, and*
> *you shall be my friend today —*
> *sleeping butterfly.*

***

> *First winter shower.*
> *The monkey too seems to want*
> *his little raincoat.*

The period at the end of the first line suggests the force of the sudden rain. It also separates the larger image of winter rain from the smaller image of the monkey shivering and trying to find shelter. It is a playful contrast, made more effective by the use of the full stop. I have tried to express this playfulness a little more pointedly by writing "his" little raincoat, which makes us feel the monkey is fairly tame, or a pet who sometimes wears clothes — in this case a rain-cape of reeds — in imitation of humans. This haiku shows the poet's deep affection for, and understanding of animals. His eye is like a painter's.

***

A sick traveller,
my dreams go running around
a withered moorland.

The first line tells us the poet is speaking about himself. He has fallen sick while on his travels, and in his delirium his dreams are uncontrollable. As in the haiku about the crow, here too I have injected movement into the second line by using "go" and the present participle "running" which denotes continuity of action, as does the word "around", in which the "a" in "around" conveys a kind of agitated, circular motion more strongly than the simple "round". I also used "around" to give me the extra syllable. As in all these translations, I have been careful to keep to the 5-7-5 construction.

It is one of the most purely impressionistic poems Bashō ever wrote, with a touch of morbid fantasy, like a Goya etching. It is utterly plain and bare, stripped of all unnecessary words and sentiments. It is desolate, like the dead landscape in which his sick dreams are rushing about so restlessly. Its pathos is true to life, and deeply moving.

We know that it was Bashō's last haiku, written when he was far from home in Saga. It was composed in Osaka shortly before he died on October 11, 1694. As Dr Samuel Johnson said, approaching death concentrates a man's mind, and we can feel this final concentration in Bashō's final work. The poem is filled with the sadness of autumn, but also with its peace.

This poem would be a fitting inscription for any memorial erected in tribute to Bashō on the 300th anniversary of his death, which was observed in 1994.

***

IMPROVEMENTS IN MY TRANSLATIONS OF BASHŌ'S POEMS

One of the interesting things about writing haiku is the way they grow. I often think they form themselve like crystals, gradually adding or subtracting material until they reach their final form. All haiku poets are familiar with this kind of organic growth of their poems from the small seed of an image, a word, an idea.

Translations of haiku, too, grow in the same way. I may think I have finally achieved a perfect translation of a haiku, but after a few days I begin to see how it could be changed for the better, so as to be even closer to the original, more harmonious in sound, more correct in form.

This happened recently with some translations I made of well-known haiku by Matsuo Bashō. The first to be revised was the one about crows in snow, and I was interested to find the Bashō made three versions of this haiku before creating a final satisfactory work of art. In the first two versions, for example, he has six syllables in what we think of as his first line, and only when he makes his third attempt does he reduce the six to five syllables.

In my revised version, I debated whether to use "falling" or "fallen" as the adjective with "snow". The idea that crows are birds we usually dislike, and that farmers hate because they eat their seeds and crops, was too difficult to express completely in English, mainly because "usually" has too many syllables. So I compromised by thinking of how the farmers must *curse* these greedy birds, instead of saying they look "beautiful" in the snow, and said they look "different." This difference comes from the stark contrast between black and white, and from the way the light from the snow illuminates the crows in a new way. So this was my final version:

> Cursèd crows — they look
> so different this morning
> in the fallen snow.

***

The changes in my Bashō translation were really changes in conception and interpetation, The same could be said about my revision of the poem about the heron. I discovered that this is a certain type of heron called *aosagi* and I felt it was important to suggest this in English by calling it a "grey heron." The grey heron is standing in water that a fairly strong evening breeze is blowing against the heron's legs in the form of waves. As first I wrote of the heron's "ankles" but then I realized that this was not suitable: Bashō was referring to the heron's long legs that were being splashed by the waves. But "legs" did not seem to me to be the best word, so I changed it to "shanks" which suggests long, thin, bony lower legs. And "splashing" sounds too weak for the force of the little waves against these sturdy shanks, so I substituted "hitting against." This was the final form of my translation, which like a true haiku semed to have beem formed like a crystal by slow accretions and rejections of materials:

> In an evening breeze
> the waves are hitting against
> a grey heron's shanks.

I deliberately used the indefinite article in the first line, to give the feelings of a wind that is somewhat vague in its intensity, neither too weak nor too strong, but just "an" evening breeze like any other of its kind and "a" instead of "the" grey heron because it is just one of many.

***

The same change from definite to indefinite article appears in my revision of the lovely haiku about the bee and the peony flower. I changed "The bee" to "A bee" to make the image more generalized: the indefinite article also seems mysteriously to increase the size of the bee. Then I felt that "leaves" was too weak for the big bee's actions as he struggles to leave the huge peony, so I decided to use a more expressive verb, "crawls out of." This required a change in the second line that enabled me to use seven syllables without employing the unnecessary word "flower":

> A bee crawls out of
> the heart of a peony —
> so reluctantly.

I think the dash after "peony" conveys a sort of hesitation on the bee's part, almost a sigh of regret. And I have been careful to say "a" peony rather than "the" peony, to make the image somehow larger and more symbolic.

It is interesting to see that Bashō also wrote a version of this haiku in which he used a butterfly instead of a bee.

***

Bashō loved butterflies. I translated one of his butterfly poems this way:

> Wake up, wake up, and
> you shall be my friend today —
> sleeping butterfly.

But the poet also liked drinking wine, so I imagined that perhaps he wanted the butterfly to wake up so that it could drink wine with him, even if it took only a small sip:

> Wake up, wake up, and
> you shall drink with me today —
> sleeping butterfly.

These are just a few examples of how haiku grow — like crystals, like plants, like creatures, and open in the end like flowers. And this is how translations, too, start to grow and develop and reach their final perfect form. In poetry especially, translation is interpretation.

We must always remember that translation of poetry is not just a translation of the words. We have to look into the poet's heart to try to see his deepest meaning, his original intention in writing the poem. Of course, it is always important to try to make a translation as close as possible to the original, without the interference of the translator's own style or personality. But a true translation is also interpretation of the poet's conception of the subject: and, perhaps, his secret intentions in writing it. In order to translate poetry on this level, the translation should preferably be made by someone who is a poet in his own right.

Only a poet can comprehend completely how another poet's mind works, even in a foreign language, for poetic intuition belongs to all true poets, whatever language they write in.

***

64

HIBINO SATOE

Upstream, there must be
a pottery-making town —
cherry blossom clouds

Ears grow sharp at night
in the new house, listening
to the wintry wind

Statue of Balzac
standing there shrouded in his
magnificent cloak

Valley stream dried up
leaving the water-mirrors
in between the rocks

Many visitors —
and yet — the quietness of
this flower temple

Right in the middle
of the ricefield, burning all
kinds of stuff — year's end

One flower petal
of Jōmon Era lotus*
blown open by the wind

Valley river sounds —
until I notice, in bloom,
the magnolias

A fossilized crab
in the deep chill of autumn
has lost both its claws

* From a 10,000 year old seed. (Jōmon Era: 10,000 BC – 300 BC.)

TAKAHA SHUGYŌ

I need that one word
acting as a wedge to start
the year's first haiku

A shooting star — not
able to use the whole length
of the vast night sky

Quicker than the snake
the stick used in its killing
starts floating away

Cracking walnuts — and
finding in the walnut shells
there are unused rooms

Lying with wife: — at
the end of the Milky Way
mother and father

Into the gauze of
the firefly cage spraying mist
makes one drop of fire

The cicada's shell
still bearing the traces of
what it has suffered

In daytime, hoisting
the sun, at night the moon
on mountain flower fields

From the skyscraper
the new green leaves of the trees
same size as parsley

LUCIEN STRYK: *CAGE OF FIREFLIES*

Modern Japanese Haiku translated by Lucien Stryk
Swallow Press/ Ohio University Press, Athens, Ohio.
118 pp. No price.   ISBN 0-8040-0977-9
ZEN, POETRY, the Art of Lucien Stryk edited by Susan
Porterfield, Swallow Press/ Ohio University Press, Athens, Ohio.
388 pp. No price.   ISBN 0-8040-0975-9

The art of haiku is not understood in Britain. In the United
States of America, though haiku are more widely appreciated and
accepted as a poetic form, they are not really understood either, and
the same could be said for most other countries outside Japan
where the writing of these three-line poems of seventeen syllables
is practised. I came to this conclusion after judging for the very
representative Japanese haiku organization, "Haiku International" a
total of over five thousand haiku submitted for competition from
Brazil, Argentine, the USA and most European countries, including
a surprisingly large number from Croatia, written in various
European languages, but chiefly in English.

The best were easily the Germans, who without exception
adhered to the 5-7-5-syllable technique. I found it curious that
some of the worst entries came from Brazil, a country with a large
number of Japanese immigrants. Perhaps having to write in
Brazilian Portuguese cramped their style. The entries from Italy,
Spain and Portugal nearly all showed a complete ignorance of the
fundamental rules of haiku writing. A few innocent children's
efforts at least had the virtue of freshness of vision. The Americans
were mostly highly professional, using what is known as the free
style — that is, ignoring syllable count and season words. The
British formed a mixed bunch of free stylers and traditionalists. But
one could find a glimmer of haiku feeling in nearly all American
and British contestants, with a few really outstandingly good
practitioners.

There is a certain amount of national sterotyping here. If the
Germans hew to the traditional forms, they are nevertheless not
strait-jacketed by them. The freeness of most American haiku is
inevitably attributed to the famous love of personal freedom in
their land, a freedom sometimes as illusory as the quality of the
free-form haiku they produce. The British sit on the fence, often

getting away with it.

But in Britain, sad to say, there is a deep resistance to the haiku. Editors shy away from them, publishers won't look at them, poetry contests explicitly state that haiku do not qualify. There is something in the minimalism and brevity of haiku that awakens deep suspicions in the British editor's breast. A significant statement was recently made to me by Michael Schmidt, editor of "P.N. Review" rejecting some translations I had made of a young German minimalist poet, Rainer Teuschl:

"I was interested to see these though, I regret to say, they do not in the end appeal to me, their thinness appearing — in the German as in the translation — a matter of eking out rather than compression. I seem to have a general problem with very short-line poems!"

(In fact, the May-June issue of the magazine included short-line poems by Richard Dove, and even a pseudo-haiku from Penny McCarthy — a real one is unthinkable. For needless to say Schmidt refuses to publish real haiku, or their satirical equivalent, *senryu*. They could be considered as short-line poems, too. But to ban poems just because their lines are short seems a lack of critical reliability, and such a blinkered view would exclude a large section of modern and indeed classical verse.)

Yet I understand his attitude. Haiku are not poems — at least, not in the sense we in the West think of poems — something solid-looking of eight or more lines. The very thought of calling a single line — the usual way of writing haiku in Japanese, sometimes adopted by westerners — a "poem" goes counter to every British poetical convention. So the word "poem" raises British expectations very high, and when confronted, perhaps for the first time, by the brevity and compactness of true haiku, the British will not admit that such a form can be classed under the heading of "poetry" or even of "light verse".

Yet these brief flashes of illumination from the haiku poet's heart and mind as he confronts the phenomena, both natural and artificial, of our one and only world are poems in their own right. They have simply been conceived in a different way from western works. The haiku poet has cast a different, oblique eye at our daily life and listened with a differently-tuned ear to the immortal whisperings in every human soul. That eye and ear belong to the universal language of all poetry, in whatever language it is written. Just because it is different from what the British expect of poetry — drab domestic/provincial academic/ limp love/feeble feminist/coyly humorous versifying — does not disqualify it in the ranks of literary skill and feeling.

To translate poetry well, the the translator should also be a poet, and a poet familiar with the cultural background of the poet he is translating. Lucien Sryk is one of those American writers who come crowned with research grants, endowments and fellowships, and he has held two visiting lectureships in Japan. But are his own poetry and his own knowledge of Japan sufficient to make him a good translator? He has been helped in his *Penguin Book of Zen Poetry* and in his most recent collection, *Cage of Fireflies: Modern Japanese Haiku* by two Japanese scholars: yet Lucien Stryk's name alone appears on the covers and on the title pages. This kind of collaboration can work quite well between two poets who know something of one another's language, but the results in the end always depend on the quality of the translating poet. The results in Lucien Stryk's case show a lax American approach to the art of haiku, and its accompanying cuteness of tone.

That cuteness can be found all over his introduction, which includes a long and pointless imaginary conversation, not between modern poets but between the masters of the classical haiku Bashō, Issa, Buson and — the only one who might qualify as "modern" — Masaoka Shiki (1867-1902). They quaff saké with Stryk and form a mutual admiration society quoting each other's haïkaï and putting forth banal views of what haiku should be in the typical American conversational style of "Sesame Street". It all ends like this:

Basho, Buson and Issa bow their heads, exclaim in unison: That strikes a chord!

Shiki: Yes, in spite of all you fear, from time to time art needs resuscitation, a kick in the pants! Let us drink a final toast to those yet to come, who will learn something from each one of us. To haiku!

Sun sets over Hagi-no-Tera as we leave the garden. Trailing my friends, I glance back one last time at the memorial stones, whisper: To haiku!

And what was it that struck the chord in the three classic poets? A haiku by a minor "modern" writer, Kashō (who is given six haiku in the second volume of R.H. Blyth's *A History of Haiku*):

> Into the cage of
> fireflies, mostly dead,
> I send a breath.

The original runs: *Okata wa/ shinikeru hotaru/ kago wo nurasu* And Blyth's translation reads pretty much the same as Stryk's:

> Blowing moisture
> Into the cage of fireflies,
> mostly dead.

Stryk begins his Introduction with this haiku, followed by:

Each year as darkness comes alive with sparkles, I remember the night my son handed me a jar of fire-flies, confident that I could turn their glow back on. I hadn't come across the poet Kasho yet. I wish I had, for this poem on the cage of fireflies might have offset a small boy's disappointment with his father.

How touching! But this appeal to family sentiments has nothing to do with the spirit of true haiku. It is a kind of emotional hostage-taking.

Blyth has a fine ear for poetry, but he was no more of a poet in his translations than Stryk is, though he was more accurate. "I send a breath" would not be sufficient to revive dying fireflies. What they need is a gentle mist of water sprayed from the mouth (*nurasu*) in the same way as bonsai growers and florists in Japan refresh their delicate plants. The misty spray is able to penetrate the fine gauze walls of the firefly "cage". Stryk's son's insects were in a jamjar — no wonder they were dead and dying — and a blast from Stryk's mouth would be all that was needed to finish them off. This is just one example of the general sloppiness of Stryk's work.

The subtitle "Modern Japanese Haiku" is inaccurate too, for most of the poets represented here are long dead. However, their work can be considered "modern" in contrast with the classical haiku poets, and modernism in haiku can be said to have started with Shiki, who was a severe critic of the poetry of his day as well as an innovator in the form. Though he also introduced baseball to Japan, his modernism is not as modern as one would expect from that, or from his criticism. As Blyth points out, Buson is often more modern than the moderns, with his pictorial realism:

> A sudden shower;
> the line of tied-up horses, —
> Their hindquarters frisk about!

Blyth has added that superfluous exclamation mark that today's western haiku poets often use in a fruitless attempt to enliven a dead final line, but his translation is more complete than Stryk's:

> Sudden rain —
> rows of horses
> twitching rumps.

Yūdachi is just one of the many Japanese words used to describe all the varieties of rain: it means a sudden, short, perhaps violent evening shower, not just sudden rain, and its effect upon horses would be more forceful than a mere twitch. And in writing about noble animals like horses, "hindquarters" is preferable to the all-too-human "rumps". Stryk's English vocabulary lacks both precision and sensitivity.

Coming to later poets, those born mainly in the last decades of the 19th century, we have Shiki's followers Takahama Kyoshi and his contemporary Kawahigashi Hekigotō. They were still writing the formal 5-7-5-syllable style, but Stryk does not respect this pattern in English. Proponents of "free-form" haiku claim that English syllables are not the same as Japanese ones. And of course come Japanese haiku poets do not use seventeen syllables. But syllables are syllables in whatever language they are spoken, so if the Japanese poet has used seventeen syllables, why not try to use seventeen in English — without padding? As Auden once said to me: "What's the fun in haiku of you don't respect the rules?" (He himself, in his "Shorts", used seventeen syllables though distributing them randomly over his three lines).

Nearly all the haiku in Stryk's book are in seventeen syllables, but he reduces them to as litttle as ten or even seven: compare with my version —

With spring leaves,	Summer leaves all round.
my child's	My child's milk teeth are starting
new teeth.	to come out just now.

71

In that haiku there is an example of another mistake: Stryk ignores the tradition of *kigo* or "season word" which is essential in all formal haiku: the spring leaves are in fact summer ones. (He does not seem to know that the author of this poem, Nakamura Yusatao, is dead (1901-1983).)

In another of Kusatao's works, he misplaces the word "warm":

(19 syllables in the original — and in mine):

Autumn sun —	My dead friend seemed to
dead friend's hand	put his hand on my shoulder —
warm on my shoulder	in the warm autumn sunlight.

Dakotsu (1885-1962) is represented by four haiku only, all translated superficially and/or erroneously: compare with my own —

Death at last —	Life comes to an end
little by little	leaving smells of medicine
fading of medicine odors.(*sic*)	and the body cold.

(Here Stryk has missed out an important part of the haiku — the cold corpse)

Mountain	Dew on taro leaves
shadowing mountain	the whole range of the mountains
dew on Taro leaf.	collecting shadows.
The iron wind-chime	Forgotten — rusty
rings	iron windbell suddenly
autumn in.	pings in autumn wind.
Into the nostrils	Dead body lying
of the corpse,	with the autumn wind blowing
autumn wind	into its nostrils.

(Though the originals vary slightly in syllable count, I have usually employed the regular seventeen syllables. I have been helped in my readings of the originals by a Japanese friend who is a haiku poet).

In a "Note", Stryk tells us: "... Noboru Fujiwara ... asked me to translate with him some pieces by his haiku master, the leader of the Tenrō (Sirius) Haiku School, Seishi Yamaguchi. I found myself becoming increasingly interested in modern haiku, and while reworking the pieces done with Takashi Ikemoto, and with the Seishi Yamaguchi poems in hand, I thought I might put together a modern collection one day." So one expects a great deal of his versions of Seishi (who died in 1993 aged 92). But here again, the translations are lacking in the rhythm of the originals. Seishi often varied the number of syllables in his haiku, and this one has 5-5-5:

Praying mantis	With a crisp sound the
straddling a wasp —	praying mantis eats
how crisp each bite.	the face of a wasp.

Stryk avoids the syllable pattern, and omits an important detail.

Seishi again: three lines of 5-6-5 syllables:

Dangling in	The end of a red
summer river,	iron chain soaking in
a red iron chain	the summer river.

The Mangajin selection of three hundred Seishi poems, *The Essence of Modern Haiku* (Box 6668, Marietta, Georgia 30065) has much better translations by Tadashi Kodaira and Alfred Marks, (though these still have their imperfections) and the great advantage of the book is that the haiku are given in Japanese, romaji and English, with often enlightening notes on each poem by the poet himself. By comparison, Stryk's little books are lamentably thin and amateurish.

Zen, Poetry, the Art of Lucien Stryk on the other hand is almost comically ponderous. It collects selections from Stryk's poetry and prose, with a section of learned essays on his work, and a list of his collected works, around thirty-five in number to date. Stryk's own poems are as weak and woolly and cute as his translations, and his essays on Zen would make many a Japanese smile with the tolerance that fatally marks their acceptance of unworthy English translations of their poetry, a tolerance dating from the 'Fifties when the Japanese were only too glad to find foreigners taking an interest in their literature, and so were prepared to overlook misapprehensions and mistakes. But that is no longer the case, and translations like those of Lucien Stryk will no longer do. He, too, needs a kick in the pants. Then the British might begin to appreciate the art of haiku.

All along the street,
even at night, the tree leaves
keep on falling fast

Takano Sujū

The abbot's quarters —
from the overhanging eaves
a spring butterfly

Takano Sujū

Another person
also starts cutting the reeds
in the far distance

Takano Sujū

The chysanthemums
burning — among the flames
one flower opening

Nomura Toshirō

The roots of grasses
are reaching deep down into
the slumber of snakes

Katsura Nobuko

The fire is so warm
I am afraid I might say
something out of place

Katsura Nobuko

The cricket's winter
preparations are also
death preaparations

Azumi Atsushi

Murmuring farewell
just as they do at the end
of the French movies

Azumi Atsushi

Haiku on the moon —
writing the words down under
the light of the moon

Azumi Atsushi

No faith in people.
I'd rather put my faith in
a jack-o-lantern

Azumi Atsushi

Something sprouting up —
so far, impossible to
tell what it might be

Tamaki Makoto

The air in turmoil
pinned a butterfly on barbed
wire entanglements   Tamaki Makoto

Dead wasp in winter:
its hands and feet all curled up
against its thorax   Nomiyama Asuka

When I wake up from
a nap, I feel I've returned
from so far away   Nomiyama Asuka

The colostomy's
ever-so-gentle farting —
last month of the year   Akimoto Fujio

When I wake up from
a nap — having to watch those
who are still sleeping   Suzuki Murio

Crucifixion sounds
of hammered nails — someone starts
to cough, cough, cough, cough...   Nomiyama Asuka

The enormous kite
did not find its real soul
until the string snapped   Mutsuo Takahashi

For the birds and worms
how painful are the springtimes:
while I do nothing   Mutsuo Takahashi

Wayfaring beetle,*
how many times shall I meet you
before my journey's end?   Mutsuo Takahashi

---

*The beetle referred to here is the blister beetle (*hanmyo*) or Spanish Fly
(*lytta vesicatoria*) which in Japan is said to guide the traveller, because
of its habit of jumping ahead of him at every few steps. It is therefore a
metaphor for life's path or the Way of Zen. It is also called 'the way-
teaching beetle'.

EARTHQUAKE HAIKU

It is a pathetic paradox that such an immense natural calamity as the 1995 earthquake in Kōbe could be captured by the seventeen syllables of a haiku. Yet several Japanese poets have been doing just that,

The really remarkable thing is that they are all very old — some in their mid-nineties. In the Kōbe earthquake, it was mostly the young who managed to survive: many of the old were killed or died of exposure or shock. Therefore my personal axiom: "A haiku a day keeps the doctor away" finds fresh support in this survival, as if by a miracle, of ancient haiku poets, some of who are now living among the ruins of their homes and their precious archives.

The oldest of them is Igarashi Bansui (born 1899) who edits the haiku magazine "Kunenbo". Here is his earthquake haiku:

> Daffodils blooming
> with unquenchable vigour
> after the earthquake

in which those brave spring flowers seem to symbolize the old poet's own irrepressible haiku spirit as well as his physical endurance at the age of 96.

Nagata Kōi was born in 1900. Several of his unique haiku are to be found in my anthology. Kōi is the editor of "Kotoza". I discovered that in 1975, he wrote what can only be considered a premonitory, prophetic, visionary haiku about his home city, Kōbe:

> This year, in springtime,
> everybody went missing —
> I alone am left

The earthquake poem he wrote twenty years later runs like this:

> The body dreaming,
> feeling it is near to death —
> ruined plum blossom

76

Another Kōbe poet, Gotō Hinao, is well known for the weekly page of haiku he edits for the "Yomiuri" newspaper. He was born in 1917. His impression of the earthquake was of a world suddenly gone mad. I have interpreted that feeling of horror at the sight of a world breaking apart with the adjective "deranged" — meaning "demented" but also "disarranged":

> Splitting frozen earth,
> splitting the skies of winter —
> the deranged earthquake

Wada Gorō was born in 1917. His earthquake haiku has a touching reference to Issa's haiku about his last dwelling place on earth:

> Well —is this to be
> my home at life's end, buried
> in five feet of snow?

Wada Gorō, looking regretfully at the ruins of his house and garden buried in rubble, writes:

> I had thought this place
> would be the last home for me —
> a premature spring

Tsunehiko Hoshino is not an old poet, and does not live in Kōbe, but in a haiku that links the Kōbe earthquake with the Great Kantō Earthquake of 1923, he wrote, on the Doll Festival Day, March 3, 1995:

> This time too
> we've lost our dolls —
> the earthquake

***

THE LIFE OF HAIKU, AND THE HAIKU OF LIFE

The writing of haiku is a kind of training for life. It teaches us how to see the world around us with new eyes every day. We learn what Albert Schweitzer called "reverence for life." A haiku therefore is a gift from heaven, from the gods of creation. It is a certain vision of things, often very humble and unnoticeable. But when we write it down, it becomes an expression of the human soul in touch with the infinite.

This year, on New Year's morning, I wrote three haiku. I like to get up very early and watch the natural world awakening: it is one of the best times for haiku illumination. Here is one of the haiku I wrote:

> The reflection of
> a sparrow flying across
> the bird-bath: New Year.

After I had written it, the words reminded me of something. What was it? Then I remembered a short passage from a very great book, *The History of the English Church and People*, one of the classics of early English writing, by a saint, the Venerable Bede of Jarrow, who lived from 673 to 735 A.D. I know his life and writings well, because I was born just a few miles from his ancient church, which I often visited as a child. He is one of our local heroes.

Strangely enough, when I came to Japan and learned something about the history and literature of this land, I discovered that the venerable Bede had been writing his great work at the same period as when the ancient capital of Heijôkyô, present-day Nara, was founded. It was also the period of the *Kojiki*, *Nihonshoki*, the consecration of the Great Buddha of Nara, and of the compiling of the *Manyôshû*. This great history was written in Latin, then translated into Anglo-Saxon, then into modern English. Here is the passage which my haiku about the flight of a sparrow reminded me of:

When we compare the present life of man with that time of which we have no knowledge, it seems to me like the swift flight of a lone sparrow through the banqueting hall where you sit in the winter months...

This sparrow flies swiftly in through one door of the hall, and out through the other...

Similarly, man appears on earth for a little while, but we know nothing of what went on before this life, and of what follows...

That comparison of man's brief life on earth with the momentary flight of a sparrow through a great banqueting hall is very Japanese in its feeling for the fleeting nature of our human existence, our life that is just the flash of haiku vision. I think it is also Buddhist in feeling, and so it is very suited to the spirit of this beautiful temple. And in Britain, the month of May is dedicated to the Venerable Bede.

(At Baiokuji Temple, Nagoya, May 1993).

***

SOME MODERN EUROPEAN HAIKUESQE POETS

The Americas, both North and South, have for many years been veritable hives of haiku activity. The United States has produced several schools of haiku poets, both strictly formal and open-ended in composition, whose work appears in a profusion of small côterie magazines, usually with evocative names like "Frogpond" [1] (the best one), "Dragonfly" and "Cicada." This often undisciplined enthusiasm for the Japanese form is well established in the United States, for it can be traced to the influence of Imagist poets like Amy Lowell and Ezra Pound, and to the earlier work of their contemporaries William Carlos Williams and Marianne Moore. The last-named was to produce, to the end of her life, outstanding poems whose brilliant technique was dominated by a rigorous counting of syllables.

In South America, Japanese immigrants have played an important part in creating the present passion for haiku in Brazil, Argentina, Paraguay and Chile, where haiku are composed in both strict and free forms in Brazilian Portuguese, in Spanish and in local native dialects. In Mexico, the great poet Octavio Paz has shown continuing interest in the problems of metre posed by the haiku form. He and Jacques Roubaud, the contemporary French poet and translator of genius, were the guiding spirits in the production of *Renga*, a quadriligual verse sequence with the Italian Edoardo Sanguineti and the British Charles Tomlinson (Gallimard, 1971). Ooka Makoto, in his recent essay, "Reviving Classical Linked Poems Abroad"[2], unaccountably fails to mention this seminal work.

Nor does Ooka seem to be aware of the existence of what he calls *renshi* — "a modern variation of the medieval Japanese *renga*, which flourished in the 12th to 16th centuries, and the later *renku*, which flourished in the Tokugawa period" — in the many original English works by Sato Hiroaki and his collaborations

1. The Haiku Society of America Inc., Japan House, New York.

2. In "Japan Quarterly," April-June 1987. Vol XXXIV, No. 2. Asahi Shimbun, Tokyo.

with American and other foreign poets, including the present writer, in modern *renga* published in "Frogpond" and in an annual anthology published in Japan.[3]

Ooka's essay is chiefly concerned with the interesting development of haikai and *renga* in Germany. He mentions in particular *Poetische Perlen Renshi* (Japanese title *Shi no Shinju, Renshi*) which he composed in collaboration with Kawasaki Hiroshi, Karin Kiwus and Guntram Vesper during the Berlin art festival event "Horizonte '85", held in Berlin in June, 1985.[4] Unfortunately Ooka does not quote any examples from these "pearls of poetry".

Ooka also recalls his experiences in collaborative poetry making at Oakland University in Michigan where he was poet-in-residence, resulting in a *renshi* of 20 linked poems with Thomas Fitzsimmons, later published as a bilingual collection, *Rocking Mirror Daybreak.*[5] Further collaborations with Dutch, English, Yugoslav, Spanish, Portuguese and Japanese poets were to follow, notably the creation of a *renshi* of 17 poems improvised in the presence of an audience in the Centre Georges Pompidou in Paris. As far as I know, the results of this interesting venture have not yet been published, and as Ooka again gives us no quotations, it is impossible to evaluate the poetic and technical quality of the improvisations. For the same reason, we cannot judge the merits or otherwise of the *renshi* produced with Dutch poets at the Poetry International Festival in Rotterdam in 1986. But at least one must praise Ooka for initiating these efforts in international poetic collaboration: would that our politicians might work together for peace and understanding in the same spirit of give-and-take!

The examples I have mentioned, though few in number, will serve to indicate a very small part of the immense upsurge of interest in Japanese poetic forms in Europe. Unfortunately, I cannot include Britain, where an ingrained provincial and insular mentality rejects foreign influences, or merely regards with

3. Anthology. Ikuta Press, 1-5-3, Sumiyoshi-Yamate, Higashinada-ku, Kobe 658.

4. Franz Greno publishing house.

5. Chikuma Shobō Publishing Co., Tokyo, 1982.

amused condescension the poetic developments of "abroad". Our backward colonial prejudices and blinkered outlook on international trade and industry perpetuate themselves even in literature. Very few foreign works now have any chance of being translated and published in Britain. As for poetry, the dismal contemporary scene is dominated by a powerful academic clique that refuses to take a more open view of foreign poetic forms and idioms. So our dwindling number of poetry magazines usually stipulate, among other limiting desiderata, "no haiku", or "no *tanka*" or "no *renga.*" These Japanese forms are automatically barred from poetry contests, or actively disparaged: for example, in the Leek Poetry Festival, contestants are invited to submit poems of up to forty lines, but no more than five haiku. One or two of the smaller regional poetry magazines do occasionally publish haiku, both original and in translation, among them "Iron" and "Modern Poetry in Translation." But these are the rare exceptions to the adamant British rule, which favours mild verses on banal personal and domestic subjects.

***

Though the writing of haiku in Europe has not reached the rather dismaying proportions of a cottage industry it is acquiring in the USA, the attitude of poets and public towards Japanese forms is much more open and welcoming than in hidebound Britain.

For example, the best book on the history and the writing of haiku, a scholarly yet very readable work, is not in English but in Spanish: Fernando Rodriguez-Izquierdo y Gavala's *El Haiku Japones: Historia y Traduccion. Evolucion y triunfo del haikai, breve poema sensitivo.* [6] In its 450 pages, this thorough-going study by a professor at the University of Seville covers every aspect of the Japanese form and is at the same time an excellent anthology of haiku with perceptive and delicately-worded Spanish translations. It was this book, in which the author pays tribute to the epoch-making explorations of the haiku by Octavio Paz, that prepared the way for the explosion of haikuism in South America, helped in advance by such ground-breaking works as Gloria

6. Publicaciones de la Fundacion Juan March, Guadarrama, 1972.

Ceide-Echevarría's *El haikai en la lírica mexicana*[7] and Paz's own beautiful translations of Bashō, *Sendas de Oku (The Narrow Road to the Deep North)*[8] A fine American scholar, Gary L. Brower, was by then able to publish "The Japanese Haiku in Hispanic Poetry."[9]

In German, a noteworthy contribution was Dietrich Krusche's collection of 151 haiku, *Abschied von Japan (Farawell to Japan)*, translations of haiku, with 37 *Wortskizzen* or prose sketches, published in 1969 in the "Lyrische Hefte" (35/36). Since then, haiku in German have become very popular in both Germany and Switzerland: one of my favourite collections is Imma Von Bodmershof's *Löwenzahn: die auf 17 Silben verkürzten Haiku*, published in 1979 in Japan.[10]

It is in German that the very best translations of Bashō to date have appeared. The admirable Swiss publishing firm Amman in Zürich issued in 1994 *Hundertelf Haiku* (One Hundred and Eleven Haiku), chosen, translated and with an illuminating introduction by Ralph-Rainer Wuthenow, (3rd edition). The versions are both poetic and accurate — a rare combination in the translating of Japanese haiku. Most English versions of Bashō and other classical poets tend towards cuteness, formlessness and sheer misconception of both the surface meaning and the cultural undercurrents — where these, indeed, are not totally neglected because of the translator's ignorance and unawareness of their profound significance. (Dr. Wuthenow is preparing a second volume of classical haiku).

Krusche's work appeared around the same time as R.H. Blyth's 16th reprint of his four volumes of haiku, published in Tokyo by Hokuseido.[11] These delightful collections were best-

7. Ediciones de Andrea, Mexico 1967.

8. Translated with Eikichi Hayashira. Introduction by Paz. Barral Editores, Barcelona 1970.

9. Verlag Itadori-Hakkosho in Matsuyama, 1979.

10. "Monumenta Nipponica", XIXII, 1-2, Tokyo, 1968.

11. An anthology of Blyth's work, with biographical and literary essays by James Kirkup, *The Genius of Haiku*, was published by the British Haiku Society in 1995.

sellers, and became the bibles of the Beats and other American poets in the period from the mid-Fifties throughout the Sixties, and are still treasured by admirers of that quirky scholar. Their general influence on the appreciation of haiku all over the world has been inestimable.

The haiku poets of Portugal, Spain and Latin America are not to be confused with the Catalans whose beautiful, poetic language has a uniqute literary tradition. While the greatest poetic activity in the ancient tongue is confined to Catalonia, haiku writing has been introduced to the tiny Catalan-speaking Principality of Andorra, where I have long had my home. I first fell in love with this austere mountain region, of immense scenic beauty high in the Pyrenees when I was Professor of English Language and Literature at the University of Salamanca in the 1950's. I travelled from Bath to Salamanca by way of Andorra, taking the train as far the French border at Le Hospitalet, then by bus through Pas de la Casa and over the innumerable winding mountain roads and snowy passes down into Soldeu, Canillo, Encamp and the capital, Andorra la Vella. Little did I know that twenty years later I would regularize my passion for Andorra by becoming a permanent resident of Encamp!

Andorra has a very old literary tradition that is strong on poety, as can be seen from the *Poemes per Andorra: Antologia Poètica*,[12] and the various editions of work by local poets and Spanish Catalonians published in the captial by Edicions Serra Airosa in the Col.lecció Nívia. This small but advanturous new publishing house was the first to publish a collection of haiku in Catalan, *Haikús d'Arinsal*,[13] by a great poet writing in Catalan and Castilian, Agustí Bartra, with an Introduction by another Catalan poet, Anton Carrera, a young professor at the University of Barcelona. Bartra's epoch-making collection of haiku, the last volume he was to publish before his death, contains three sections: "*La flauta d'escorça*" (*The Flute of bark*); "*El vent*" (*The Wind*); and "*La trena infinita*" (*The infinite plait*) — 60

12. Edicio del Comu d'Andorra la Vella, Any 1981.

13. Edicions Serra Airosa. Col.lecció Nìvia. Principat d'Andorra, 1982.

haiku in all, one to a page, each section illustrated, respectively, with prints by Shoshon, Kuniyoshi and Ryuzaburo Umehara, the last showing a naked Japanese woman plaiting her long, thick black hair.

Agustí Bartra, born 1912, died in the summer of 1982, shortly after spending some months in the Andorran resort town of Arinsal, where he wrote his haiku — hence the title, *Haikús d'Arinsal*. His wife, Anna Murià, has since published a best-selling biography of her husband, *Crònica de la Vida d'Agustí Bartra*.[14]

Bartra published many volumes of poetry, beginning with *Cant Corporal (Body Song)* printed in Barcelona in 1938. He wrote in both Castilian Spanish and Catalan, and, because the Catalan tongue was banned by the Franco régime, Bartra went into exile, chiefly in Mexico, until the end of the Fascist dictatorship, when he returned to Catalonia and started publishing again in Barcelona. His work has been widely translated into French, Portuguese and Dutch, and, at the Poetry International Festival in Rotterdam in 1978, in which I was priviledged to participate, there were readings of his work in many other languages, including Finnish, Russian and Japanese. But I beleieve my translations of Bartra's haiku are the first to appear in English.

Bartra's haiku are often haikuesque — that is, showing the qualities and the spirit of haiku without slavish imitation of the rules. But always they have a genuine Japanese feeling, at the same time being highly individual in tone, subject-matter and style, using mostly imagery from Catalonia and the Pyrenees. He is scrupulous in observing the strict 5-7-5 syllable count, so I have felt it necessary to do the same in my translations. In all my translations of poetry my versions keep very close to the originals, because I am convinced that the true translator of true poetry should not immodestly push his own personality forward, but should stand back and allow the poet he is translating to speak out

14. Edicions Serra Airosa, Prinicipat d'Andorra. Col.lecció Valira, No. 1. Pròleg d'Antoni Ribera. Nota a la segona edició d'Antoni Morell.

with his own voice, his own rhythm, in his own unique way. Not all of Bartra's haiku take kindly to English: his vision and his Catalan words are sometimes so powerful, they are beyond the comparatively pallid resources of my native poetic tongue. Here are sixteen.

Alguna cosa
plora a l'herba mullada.
Enyor de cérvols.

There is something there
weeping on the dew-soaked grass —
the pining of stags.

Els eixams d'alba,
les senyeres d'úserda,
els blancs geranis!

In the swarming dawn
the streamers of alfalfa
— white geraniums!

L'aire m'habita:
dono vida a la imatge
de la nostàlgia.

Air inhabits me:
I give life to the image
of nostaliga.

Tot es sendera
per als records que anhelen
l'alta devesa.

Everything's a path
through memories that yearn for
the highest pasture.

Amb passes d'aire
camino vers campanes
que ja em somien.

With an airy stride
I bend my steps towards the bells
already calling me.

Les rels antigues:
aire, foc, terra i aigua.
Atura't, Roda!

The most ancient roots:
air, fire, earth and water.
Wheel, suspend your flight!

L'hora em decanta
a tocar un tors de bronze
amb mà de llana.

Time inclines me to
knock on a torso of bronze
with a hand of wool.

Amb mà distreta,
en passar, he tocat l'arbre.
Ara em contesta.

With an idle hand,
in passing, I knocked on the tree.
Now it answers me.

Dret moriria,
com el fum que es transforma
sense saber-ho.

Let me die standing
as smoke lets itself be changed
without knowing it.

Sóc sant d'ermita,	The hermitage's
fusta policromada	holy block of wood, painted
per mans antiques.	by ancestral hands.

I pelegrinen
els ulls de la nit vella:
cerquen l'alosa.

And all the pilgrims
the eyes of ancient night:
looking for the lark.

Martells de boira
coronen l'enyorança
de fargues mortes.

The hammers of fog
are crowning my homesickness
with fireless smithies.

He vist la dríade
de cabellera d'heura
i cara hidràulica.

I saw the dryad
her hair a mane of ivy
her face hydraulic.

Aquí, silenci,
el vol d'or de l'abella
és vaticini.

There, in the silence,
the bumble-bee's golden flight
becomes prophecy.

La llum ensenya
a l'aire que viatja
com neix la rosa.

The light is teaching
the air in its wanderings
how the rose is born

Riu riu rialla,
Arinsal de l'altura
que baixa i canta.

Riverrun laughter,
from the heights of Arinsal
tumbling and singing.

(With acknowledgements to "Translation" (Columbia University) and "Modern Haiku" (Madison, USA), where these first appeared.)

I believe that Agustí Bartra's discovery of the haiku form, which was due partly to the strong influence on his work of the poetry of Octavio Paz, will encourage other Catalan poets to compose haikuesque verses.

Certainly, the other Catalan poets I have translated have not so far shown any development of Bartra's revolutionary example. Yet in my versions of work by great Catalan poets like Joseph Vicens Foix and Salvador Espriu, both recently deceased, there are those intimate poetic touches that we find in all good poets and which recall the true haiku spirit. Espriu, in *El caminant i el mur*[15] (The Wayfarer and the Wall), prints a number of five-line poems that are not unlike *tanka* in feeling — "*tanka*esque," if I may be allowed to use the expression. But they do not go well into English, unlike the longer poems of his I have translated.

Younger, less well-known Catalan poets sometimes approach haiku brevity; Josep-enric Dalleres, Anton Carrera. The latter, in his collection *Nívia*[16] has this poem full of haiku imagery, though the form is certainly not Japanese:

> Voldria ser l'obscur destinatari
> d'un rar amor passat de contraban,
> tan trèmul com la lluna sobra l'aigua,
> tan càlid com els tints de la tardor.
> Saber que quan te'n vas ella t'espera:
> conjur terral que em faci retornar.

> I should like to be the secret receiver
> of some rare love, brought in like contraband,
> as tremulous as moonlight over water,
> as warm as tints of autumn leaves.
> Knowing that when you leave, it waits for you
> would be pledge enough to make you return to it.

Unfortunately, British poets do not have this openness towards foreign forms, and our contemporary versifiers do not have the talent to be original. The only British poet I know who has adopted a foreign form is Geoffrey Hill, who occasionally uses the brief Spanish form of the *copla*, not very well.

***

While the *haikai* and other Japanese forms are neglected by most British poets who regard such deceptive simplicity as childish, haiku, *tanka* and an extended form the cinquain (invented by an American with the improbable name of Adelaide Crapsey) are used effectively in the teaching of poetry to schoolchildren, and examples can often be found in textbooks and readers and anthologies, often written by poets who would disdain to include them in their own slim volumes.

15. Edicions 62 s/a, Barcelona, 1983 (setena edicio).

16. Edicions Serra Airosa, Principat d'Andorra, 1981.

But in France, leading contemporary poets like Jacques Roubaud and Yves Bonnefoy (who edited the famous haiku anthology published by Fayard in 1978) have shown sustained interest in the form. Roubaud has written essays on the *Manyoshu* and the *Shinkokinshu,* and in 1970 published from Gallimard his selection of 403 poems "borrowed" from the Japanese in *Mono no aware: le sentiment des choses.* He has also translated several American poets who have been interested in Zen and haiku: Cid Corman, Gary Snyder, Jack Spicer and Jerome Rothenberg among them. Under the influence of Georges Perec, Pierre Lusson and Raymond Queneau, he has been attracted to the use of mathematics and board games in the creation of new poetic forms, and has written an excellent book on *go: Petit traité invitant à la découverte de l'art subtil du go,* recently reprinted by Christian Bourgeois, but originally issued in 1969. All these influences seem to have brought him closer and closer to almost abstract Japanese forms. Like the Italian poet Andréa Zanzotto, much of his best work is fragmentary in style. Zanzotto's *Galateo, Fosféna* and *Idioma* illustrate well the Italian poet's obsessions with words as things, as fragments of mosaic, as reality seen through the multiple eyes of a fly. Roubaud, too, uses language in this disjunctive, impressionist, aleatory, reductive way — half poetry, half prose, tentative yet inevitable as the strokes of a calligrapher's brush:

> *La diction que j'expérimente   est   au contraire*
> *monotone   répétitive   imperméable   indifférente*
> *   endort et attend et récidive   la voix   reste*
> *semblable à la voix qu'elle était   dans les lieux   les*
> *moments   de la composition*

(from *Dors, précédé de Dire la Poésie.* Gallimard, 1981)

> The diction I experiment with   is   on the contrary
> monotone   repetitive   impermeable   indifferent
>   drowses and waits and has relapses   the voice   stays
> just like the voice it was   in the places   the
> moments   of composition[17]

17. All translations in this essay are by James Kirkup.

This unpunctuated passage — or rather, this passage punctuated by gaps, pauses, hesitations, silences — is typical of Roubaud's constant preoccupations with voice and translation. For him, a certain way of speaking poetry — a way that is neither poetic nor private nor public but as it were an abstracted stammering — is also a kind of translation from the personal to the general, the individual to the anonymous mass. He makes references to Japanese poetry:

Ancient Japanese poetry had a sung mode of diction　which was not music　which acted as a support to the voice speaking
　poetry　and so it was that one could say that even
when alone　one was composing　as we are taught in that
description　by Teika the Great　singing all alone　his
poems　in the palace　in winter　by the despairing light
of his lamp　in darkness

Such meditations lead naturally to the stripped, brief verses of the second part of the book, which has the title *Dors* (Sleep), in such a poem as

je m'éveille	*i awaken*
et je vois	and i see
dans	in
la nuit	the night
je vois	i see
que	that
je suis seul	i am alone

and the themes of silence and repetition appear thus, haikuesque:

un silence	*a silence*
chaque bruit	each sound
une	once
fois.	only.
l'eau, cent.	water, hundreds.

90

The reiterations of archaic Japanese poetry are to be found, too, recalling the great ritual chants of the *Kojiki*:

chant du soleil

les rayons du soleil fuient

les rayons du soleil fuient

les rayons jaunes du soleil fuient

les rayons jaunes du soleil fuient

fuient

chant of the sun

the rays of the sun fleeting

the rays of the sun fleeting

the yellow rays of the sun fleeting

the yellow rays of the sun fleeting

fleeting

The final poem in *Dors* is one of only two lines:

chant des nuages	*chant of the clouds*
les nuages	the clouds
changent	changing

Roubaud's latest volume, *Quelque chose noir* (*Some thing black*) published by Gallimard in 1986, is an extended mourning meditation for the death of the poet's wife, Cleo. Here the lines are longer, with an appropriate addition of weight that is however never solemn. Grief causes the poet to utter stifled cries that emerge almost in spite of himself from emotional numbness, dumbness. It is significant that the spaces between words in *Dors* here become shorter and shorter, until their place is taken by full stops or periods that neither mark the end of sentences nor the beginning of others, for there are no capitals; another fragmentation effect. This "minimal" poem from *Dors* is pure haiku:

une branche	a branch
frotte	rubs
la fenêtre	the window
et puis	and then
frotte	rubs
la fenêtre	the window

Compare this with the more expansive minimalism of two long lines from *Quelque chose noir*:

Je te regardais. le sombre. le noir. le noir rangé sur le point vivant. de ton ventre.

Je tapais du pied sur l'herbe. les douze pigeons s'élevaient d'un mêtre puis se reposaient.

I was looking at you. darkness. blackness. the blackness laid on the living pivot of your belly.

I would stamp my foot on the grass. the twelve pigeons would rise up one metre and then settle again.

These phrases, and slight variations of them, are repeated several times in this "Composition rhythmique abstraite pour pigeons et poète."

Throughout the book, we find a mixture of Roubaud's former typographical eccentricities and his rhythmical effects. But though the minimalist verses are often longer, they are usually composed of enigmatic, minimalist lines — haiku seeds and essences — until the very last sections where the poems have titles like "Aphasia," "Non-life" and "Nothing."

In this respect , Roubaud takes after his undoubted master, René Char, whose most representative work of the 'Sixties was *Fureur et Mystère* (*Fury and Mystery*) containing among other items the reprinted plaquette of the immediate post-war years 1945-1947, *Le Poète Pulvérisé* (*The Pulverised Poet*) a very significant title when one considers the "pulverised" poetry and art of France herself still pulverized by traumatic war, defeat, resistance and collaboration with the Nazis. Char's work is a mixture of cryptic poetic prose, which, despite its enigmatic tone, seems based on deeply personal experiences, and abstruse, hermetic ejaculations or esoteric epigrams that are often, in their haecceity impervious to hermeneutics, close to Greek fragments and "abstract" haiku:

Celui qui se fie au tornesol ne méditera pas dans la maison.

He who puts his trust in the sunflower shall not meditate within the house.

Dans la boucle de l'hirondelle un orage s'informe, un jardin se construit.

In the swallow's loop a thunderstorm takes shape, a garden is laid out.

Another contemporary French poet who uses fragmentation and image-diffraction is Philippe Jaccottet, whose work often approaches the profound abstraction of music. (In his latest collection, *Pensées sous les Nuages* — *Thoughts under the Clouds*, — a whole section is devoted to the music of Henry Purcell). While Jaccottet is more conventional than Roubaud in his typography and punctuation, he is sometimes much more vivid in his apprehension of the world in haiku-like visions:

On voit les écoliers courir à grands cris
dans l'herbe épaisse du préau.

You can see the schoolchildren running with loud cries
in the thick grass of the yard.

and:

Et dans le jour encore gris
courent ici et là comme la crête d'un feu pâle
les branchages neufs des tilleuls...

And in the still-grey morning
like the crest of a pale fire there run
the fresh branchings of the limes.

Jaccottet uses the image of a weaver and a loom very effectively to suggest the work of the poet, and at the end of the sequence on Henry Purcell come these four superb haikuesque lines:

Tu es assis
devant le métier haut dressé de cette harpe.

Même invisible, je t'ai reconnu,
tisserand des ruisseaux surnaturals.

You are seated
before the high loom of this harp.

Even invisible, I could recognize you,
weaver of supernatural streams.

***

I should like to end this essay by introducing to Japan some of the haiku or haikuesque poems of the great modern Greek poet George Seferis, who in 1963 was the first Greek to win the Nobel Prize for literature. He first became interested in the arts of Japan in Paris, in 1922, when with his friend Poniridis he visited an exhibition of Japanese works at the Grand Palais. Of course, under the influence of the Imagists, the haiku form was already in vogue in Europe, though practised by only a few poets like Claudel. Greek poetry is often fragmentary since classical times.[18]

Seferis published sixteen haiku in his 1940 collection *A Book of Exercises*: they are dated 1931 and 1932. Twenty-four further haiku were printed in the two volumes of his *Journal*, including a translation of Bashō's poems about a grasshopper chirping under a dead warrior's helmet, later reprinted in his second volume of essays. These have all been translated into English.[19]

18. See *The Greek Anthology*, the poems of Sappho.
19. *Poems*, Atlantic, Brown, Little, 1960. Translated by Rex Warner.
Collected Poems 1924-55, Cape, 1969. Translated by Keely & Sherrard.
A Poet's Journal: Days of 1941-51, Harvard U.P., 1974. Translated by Athan Anagnostopoulos.
The King of Asine and Other Poems, John Lehmann, 1948, has unfortunately long been out of print.

Sefaris often gives his haiku titles, usually indicating the place referred to in the poem. for example, in the haiku here translated by me, about the empty chairs in the public park, the title is "In the Museum Park." (Presumably the Jardins des Tuileries and the Louvre.) Others, not translated here, are entitled "Venice", "Geneva", "Omonoia" (the name of the great "Harmony" square in central Athens). Others are given more literary figures like "Wrinkles", "Cinemathans", "Consecration", "Sick Erinys" and "New Destiny." The first in my series of five haiku by Seferis has the title "Poetic Art." I have preferred to omit these adventitious titles, beleiving that haiku should be self-sufficient, as indeed those of Seferis nearly always are, requiring no extraneous explanations, though haiku with place names are not unknown in Japanese.

Five syllables — then
seven and five. Just look there!
All those butterflies.

Πέντε συλλαβές;
κι ἐφτὰ καὶ πέντε. Δές τις!
Οἱ πεταλοῦδες.

What do you think they're
up to, those almond trees
blossoming in snow?

Κάτι πιστεύουν
οἱ μυγδαλιὲς ποὺ ἀνθίσαν
μέσα στὸ χιόνι.

Boat's drifting circles —
What's happening to the rudder?
— And not one seagull.

Τὸ δοιάκι τί ἔχει ;
Ἡ βάρκα γράφει κύκλους
κι οὔτε ἕνας γλάρος

Statues returned to

95

a different museum —
the park's empty chairs.

Ἄδειες καρέκλες
τ'ἀγάλματα γυρίσαν
στ' ἄλλο μουσεῖο

To think of one's death
is easy enough — but not
one's own dead body.

Εὔκολο ποὺ εἰναι
νὰ ιδεῖς τὸ θάνατό σου.
Μὰ τοῦ κορμιοῦ σου.

I feel that modern Japanese haiku poets — and indeed many western practitioners of the art — could learn much from these experiments in form and content. In all these modern European poets we find a poetic spirit which has something in common with the spirit of haiku. True poetry is always poetry, whatever its form or the language it is composed in, and so poetry itself, like music, can be regarded as essentially an international means of communication. We can appreciate the sounds of a well-read poem even if we do not understand the words, as I have discovered when listening to the readings by modern Russian and Arab poets, who read poetry supremely well, with a persuasive passion.

Yet haikuesque poems will always be something different from native haiku. The European poets are interested in an adventurous exploration of the possibilities of the form, which in Japanese is sometimes too limiting, or even not minimal enough, or hampered by what to a westerner often seem arbitrary rules for "season words," *renga* composition and so on.

The main thing is to have an open mind, to have a willing spirit and a desire to renew ancient forms as well as to preserve them. This is what I believe my European poets are contributing to universal understanding, though the spirit of haiku, which is the universal spirit of all poetry.

SOME HAIKUESQUE POEMS BY OCTAVIO PAZ

The great Mexican poet is well known for his *renga* sequence written in collaboration with Eduardo Sanguinetti (Italian), Jacques Roubaud (French) and Charles Tomlinson (English). This multilingual effort was praiseworthy even though it was not entirely successful: none of the other poets could match Paz in verbal brilliance and passionate emotion.

Paz has often shown a preference for the very long, Whitmanesque line in massively-structured major poems like "El Rio" and "Mutra" in his 1948-1957 collection *La Estación Violenta* or his homage to Sade, "El Prisoniero" in *Calamidades y Milagros* (1948) and many other works collected in *Libertad bajo Palabra* (1960 – many reprints).

Yet in earlier works like *Puerta Condenada* (1938-1946) both the lines and the poems are of a more reasonable length, and in collections from the 'Forties and 'Fifties like *Condición de Nube* (1944) and *Piedras Sueltas* (1955) there are many much shorter poems, some of only three lines approaching the haiku form; in the former, there is a kind of *renga* sequence on insomnia, "Apuntes del Insomnio" and a three-line poem with typical haiku feeling for birds:

> *Retorica*
> *Cantan los pájaros, cantan*
> *sin saber lo que cantan:*
> *todo su entendimiento es su garganta.*

> *Rhetoric*
> Sparrows singing, singing
> not knowing what they are singig:
> all their brains are in their throats.

In the latter collection, "Lección de Cosas" (Object Lesson) there is a fine sequence of mostly three-line poems, followed by two sequences ("En Uxmal" and "Piedra Sueltas" — "In Uxmal" and "Loose Stones") of six and seven mainly three-line verses.

Though these three-liners cannot strictly be considered as haiku — there is no formal syllable-count, no"season word" — a certain apprehension of haiku feeling is evident. We remember that Paz was Mexican ambassador to India during the 'fifties, and visited Japan. From the last-named sequence let us take No. 5:

> *Ante la Puerta*
> *Gentes, palabras, gentes.*
> *Dudé un instante:*
> *la luna arriba, sola.*

> *Outside the Door*
> People, words, people.
> Wait a momant:
> the moon up there, alone.

It is the classic haiku effect of contrast between the human or animal world and something high above them, calm and unaffected by our petty concerns — clouds, stars, cherry blossoms, the moon, the song of birds and so on.

For Paz, the word *palabra* is all-important, but it cannot really be adequately translated simply as a "word" because, like the French *parole*, it also signifies the gift of speech. In a prose work of 1949, *Trabajos del poeta*, Paz writes about *palabra* as the natural expression of his countrymen and of his poetry:

> *Y tú, viento que soplas del Pasado, sopla con fuerza, dispersa estas pocas sílabas y hazlas aire y transparencia. ¡Ser al fin una Palabra, un poco de aire en una boca pura, un poco de agua en unos labios ávidos!*

> And you, wind blowing from the Past, blow with all your might, scatter these few syllables and turn them to air and clarity. Be finally a Word, a little breath in a pure mouth, a little water on our parching lips!

Those "few syllables" return in the poet's latest collection, *Arbol Adentro* (1987) (*The Tree Within*), in a sequence of six haiku on the poet Matsuo Bashō's simple country dwelling, called

Bashō-an, and which gives the title to the sequence. In a note, Paz tells us that he visited this exquisitely plain little cottage with his wife in 1984, on the outskirts of Kimpukuji Temple in Kyoto, where Bashō spent a short period in somewhat mysterious circumstances. The place has been named after Bashō: it was re-discovered by another important haiku poet, Buson, in 1760, who found it in a state of extreme dilapidation one hundred years after Bashō had lived there, and reverently restored it. The original Bashō-an, however, was in Edo (present-day Tokyo) at Fukagawa, built for Bashō near the river Sumida by one of his admirers. Today one can visit the nearby classic garden called Hyakkaen or Garden of One Hundred Flowers, laid out in 1801 by Kiku-u Sawara, a rich landowner with literary leanings. Some of Bashō's poems are carved on monuments in this delightful garden, once the favourite haunt of Edo poets.

In the original Spanish, the six haiku are not in strict form. However, as I was translating them, I found the poet's lines falling quite naturally into the 5-7-5 syllables of the traditional verse:

BASHŌ AN

The world contained in
seventeen syllables: you
in this little hut.

Tree trunks and straw thatch:
through the gaps between them enter
Buddhas and insects.

Created of air
from among pine trees and rocks,
the poem springing.

Woven together —
vowels and consonants build
the house of the world.

Bones of centuries,
pains already rocks, mountains:
here they have no weight.

99

What I have to say
contained in barely three lines:
hut of syllables.

In the same volume there are two three-line poems that can also be considered as haiku because of their traditional subject matter. Again the form is not strict, and in my translations I have not attempted to create poems of seventeen syllables because the originals are already so beautifully spare. They both have titles, a practice also favoured in his haiku by the Greek poet Sefaris, but one that is rarely found in Japanese.

DAWN

On the sand,
calligraphies of birds:
memories of wind.

CALM

Moon, hourglass:
the night is running out,
the hour brightens.

It is possible that Octavio Paz was attracted towards haiku form in part because it reminded him of the Spanish *copla*. Of course, the *copla* usually has four lines, and is an altogether more popular form than the haiku, perhaps because of its often mocking ballad-like tone more akin to the satirical *senryu*. All in all, Paz has made a notable contribution to the creation of haiku in the westerm world.

But because of their lack of formal structure, I would qualify his three-line verses as "haikuesque" though they often exhibit true haiku feeling — something possessed by most good poets, whatever their language or nationality.

SOME MODERN TURKISH HAIKU AND HAIKUESQUE POEMS

The little finger is called
"sparrow finger" in Turkish.
Does your hand twitter?   Feyyaz Fergar

Every morning after breakfast
I commit suicide as the best way to test
eternity — and also to have something to do.
         Feyyaz Fergar

He has glow-worms in his brain.
No wonder he looks so dazzled. Feyyaz Fergar

To consult a pebble you
must unlearn many landscapes,
discard many seasons.   Feyyaz Fergar

Two blind men
watering the same
flower — Help!   Feyyaz Fergar
   (Translated by James Kirkup)

Bury me not in garrulous cemeteries.
A bit of silence
goes well with a long death. Ismail Uyaroglu
   (Translated by Feyyaz Fergar)

If only I could stop this passer-by —
If only I could tell him to treasure
His few remaining steps Necip Fazil
   (Translated by Feyyaz Fergar)

Do not touch, do not disturb
this madness in me. Do not torture
secrets that cannot see me. Necip Fazil
   (Translated by Feyyaz Fergar)

My eyes
somehow
remind me of you.   Edip Cansever
                                (Translated by Feyyaz Fergar)

I've left death threadbare.
I'm on my way   Ithan Berk
                                (Translated by Feyyaz Fergar)

Eat quinces.
God will take note of that as well.   Ithan Berk
                                (Translated by Feyyaz Fergar)

Tulip, how are you?
Where are you off to like that?   Ithan Berk
                                (Translated by Feyyaz Fergar)

(Feyyaz Fergar is a modern Turkish poet and translator
who worked for many years in the Turkish Section of the
BBC in London. He writes in English, French and Turkish.
His first book, *Gestes à la Mer*, was published by Grey
Walls Press in London in 1943, with an Introduction by
James Kirkup. He is adviser to the poetry magazine
"Core," and has translated Bashō into Turkish.)

***

TWO HAIKU BY RAINER MARIA RILKE

I found the two poems that follow in a small collection of poetic fragments by Rilke, published in a bilingual edition entitled *Chant Eloigné* by Verdier, (Paris, 1990). Both poems are about musical instruments: grand piano and flute.

The poems are not strictly speaking haiku in form, but as I was working on their translation into English from the German I discovered that they could be expressed in seventeen syllables, though season words are lacking.

The first poem was written by the poet in the guest-book of Baronin Gisela von Hess-Diller:

> Wie dunkeln und rauschen im Instrument
> > die Wälder seines Holzes. (1906)

> How they darkle and
> rustle in the instrument —
> its framework's forests.

The second poem belongs to Rilke's Paris period, when he was associated with the sculptor Rodin, and was written in 1910. The subject is an antique Greek flute, possibly one of the props Rodin used for his sculptures:

> O Kreuzweg meines Mundes
> o Lippenbinde, o Flöte,
> die den Atem mir entzweit.

> O my mouth's crossways,
> o lip closure, o flute that
> sunders breath in me.

These haiku-like fragments remind us of the importance of music in the work of Rilke, in particular his *Sonnets to Orpheus* belonging to his later period. And we remember the close of an earlier "Love Song":

> ...Upon what instrument are we taut-spanned,
> and what musician has us in his hand?

Here the "instrument" is a violin. In the first poem I have assumed it is a grand paino. Jane Austen several times uses the word "instrument" to denote a piano: for example, in chapter 8 of *Persuasion*.

SEVEN HAIKU BY ZHU HAO

(from the sequence "Salt")

from across the shade
of pear blossoms in noon light
comes chess-sound sometimes

sawmill in drizzle
the fresh smell of new-cut wood
behind the wet breeze

when I am in drink
would pear blossoms fall as rain
and cover my sleep?

archery practice:
the sound of bowstring quivers
in the freezing wind

in folds of the skirt
cold scent of rose and jasmine
moving with her step

lake is a large eye
reflecting the sunset clouds
thousands of white cranes

the warm light of dawn
filling all the icicles
on bare branch of oak

(from the Chinese)

***

YANNIS RITSOS : A MODERN GREEK POET WITH HAIKU FEELING

We usually associate Greek poetry with the epics of Homer, traditionally regarded as the author of the *Iliad* and the *Odyssey*. However, there is also a long tradition of Greek verse that takes the form of epigrams and fragments. The most famous examples of these are to be found in *The Greek Anthology*. based upon the 10th century *Anthology* of Cephalas of Constantinople, re-arranged by Maximus Planudes in 1301 and first published at Florence in 1494. The epigram is a short poem ending with a witty or ingenious thought, thus:

> Sir, I admit your general rule,
> That every poet is a fool:
> But you yourself may serve to show it,
> That every fool is not a poet.

This little verse, variously attributed to Coleridge, Pope, Prior and Swift, has some of the elements of haiku or *senryu* — brevity and a surprise ending — though it lacks the profound love of an observation of nature to be found in the Japanese form. Greek fragments of poetry are like fragments of ancient sculpture, and are sometimes erotic; sometimes philosophical, like the inscription in the temple at Delphi — "Nothing in excess" — a motto that could be applied to the writing of haiku. Sappho, Anacreon and Menander are among the best-known of the poets in *The Greek Anthology*, whose verse is often fragmentary and yet whose poetic spirit has inspired and influenced many British and European poets.

Yannis Ritsos may be regarded as one of the fathers of contemporary Greek poetry. He was born in 1909, and he has lived through troubled times of war, famine, exile and dictatorships. Towards the end of the 1970's Ritsos, who, because of his political views, was often compelled to leave Athens and go into semi-exile, spent the summer on the isalnd of Samos, where he has a small country house, near the picturesque little port of Karlovassi. It was in this house, from August to September of 1979, that Yannis Ritsos composed his first collection of "fragments" — poems of one line, under the title *MONOXOPDA* or "*One String Songs*" which have now finally been beautifully translated into French by Dominique Grandmont under the title *Sur une Corde* and published by the small Editions Solin.

It is an enchanting collection of one-line poems — though some of them are so short they could be called genuine archaic "fragments" while others are rather longer than a single line. As Japanese haiku were originally composed in this single-line form, rather than in the three-line form of 5, 7 and 5 syllables now so familiar in the West, the comparison with the "one string" verses of Ritsos is inevitable. The poet has recently declared himself to be weary of poetry and poets and critics. But the practice of these one-line poems seems to have restored his faith in himself and in his art. Some of these poems express vividly the strong, independent, rebellious and non-conformist nature of this great poet:

This monument, built of all the stones that were cast at me.

and

Sunday bells are only for children and old folk.

Yet he has a marvellous sense of humour, full of ancient, pithy wisdom, and his one-liners often read like proverbs:

Your kite is broken? Keep the string.

Poetry invented the world. The world has forgotten it.

You must make a lot of holes in a reed to make it sing.

The same regret for what you have done, also for what you have not done.

Poetry did not always have the first word. But the last, always.

One gets the impression of a shrewd and sharp-witted old poet enjoying himself jotting down whatever comes into his head. Some of these jottings seem to show him laughing slyly at himself:

It's raining and I've opened my umbrella to keep my old statue from getting wet.

If I cannot make you see it, it's because I did not have it.

The intangible — I give it all entirely. But no one takes it.

That last line sounds like a wry comment on today's popular indifference to poetry.

Many of these short poems are like rapid sketches drawn with a single stroke of a brush, almost in a certain style of oriental calligraphic painting:

The egg shining in the mother's hand.

A mountain, two apples, three soldiers.

Sad little village, with two chairs in the street.

The mountain, the sea and a naked girl behind the sunflowers.

Every second, a tree, a bird, a chimney, a woman.

Maize, grapes, a donkey and the sky.

Big proletarian moon over the sleeping town.

Outside the locked house, winds, smoke, chairs.

This is the type of poem which I started experimenting with in the early 1970's, under the influence of Gyomindo Ikehara's one-line haiku magazine "Shikai," published in Nagoya, and now, alas, defunct. I still remember the wonderful day when Gyomindo, a frail but sprightly old gentleman, came to visit me in my house in Nagoya, and asked me to contribute some one-line English poems to "Shikai." At once I saw the possibilities of this unique form, and from that day on, I have rarely passed a day without getting in shape for the writing of longer poems by practising some one-liners. A selection of these was published in 1980 by Kyoto Editions (my own little publishing firm) under the title *Dengonban Messages* and predictably met with the amused contempt and good-humoured condescension of British reviewers. I sent a copy of the book to Yannis Ritsos, but I do not know if he received it. At any rate, it is interesting that we should both have been writing one-liners about the same time. My little book may even have inspired him to publish his own collection of one-liners.

While I was translating these pellucid and mysterious verses, I kept remembering Dominique Grandmont's statement in his introduction: "To translate... is to betray one's own language in favour of the original." I have always tried, when writing translations in English, especially of poetry, to give the English the characteristic intonations, rhythms and idioms of the original, rather than to turn the foreign poet into an out-and-out Britisher. So when I was "Englishing" Ritsos after my own fashion, I found that I was putting many of his one-liners into a distinctly Japanese 17-syllable form. Indeed, some of them naturally fell into the 5-7-5 disposition of syllables, so that the English took on a sort of Japanese-Greek conformation:

> Cheap hotel. Candle
> on the washbasin. Hidden
> voices in the night

> Jasmin petal in
> a glass of water — to what
> far lands do you take me.

> On the chair beside
> his bed, the miner has placed
> the old alarm-clock.

> A slim crescent moon.
> The heroes urinating
> at the street corner.

> It's when I'm with you
> (and not when I am alone)
> that I am alone.

> The word, that passes
> with such difficulty from
> blood to poetry.

> If from time to time
> you do not close your eyes, you
> will never grow up.

> Dumb conversation
> between the lighthouse keeper
> and the sinking ship.

> You have glimpsed the sky's
> immensity, through the bright
> keyhole of a star.

I even found that I had written as one line a poem that divides itself perfectly into 5-7-5 syllables:

> The same regret for
> what you have done — also for
> what you have not done.

I have always thought that the Japanese are the Greeks of the Orient, and the Greeks the Japanese of the West. One only has to observe groups of Japanese tourists in Greece: they look so free and so happy, surrounded by the natural courtesy, kindness and hospitality of the Greeks, so very different from the treatment the Japanese receive in other European lands. So perhaps it is not surprising that a contemporary Greek poet should go so well into Japanese forms.

Yannis Ritsos ends his little book with this indication to the reader: "These melodies on a single string are my keys. Take them." It is an invitation all European poets, and especially our hidebound British ones, would do well to take. As Philip Sherrard wrote in his book *The Marble Threshing-Floor* (Valentine, Mitchel. London 1956): "— the true voice of poetry, because the most aware of the deepest realities, has been actually singing all this time, largely unheard, in Greece." Unfortunately he says nothing about Ritsos in this book, which deserves updating and reprinting. But there can be no doubt about the importance of Yannis Ritsos in the world of contemporary poetry, as could be proved by the numerous tributes to him recently in Paris during a wonderful week of Greek poets speaking their own work at the Maison de la Poésie, from which Ritsos was absent only because of old age. This series of lively encounters, called "*Les Belles Étrangères*", between French and foreign poets and prose writers, has included a remarkable and unforgettable presentation of writers from Ireland, from both sides of the border. There was something Greek in their freshness and enthusiasm, but so far it was the Greeks who made the deepest and most lasting impression: as Sherrard pointed out thirty-five years ago: "...nothing has been so striking as the growth and fecundity of (Greece's) intellectual life... With a fresh, unexplored language, and with the living stream of a demotic tradition on which to draw, poet has succeeded poet with an insistence that is astonishing." And their work is international in appeal, as these Greek-Japanese poems of Yannis Ritsos demonstrate.

OSAKI HOSAI: *PORTRAIT D'UN MOINEAU À UNE PATTE*

Traduction et adaptation par Makoto Kemmoku et Alain Kervern

Editions Folle Avoine. 72pp. 70F. ISBN 2-86810-067-8

This brief "portrait of a one-legged sparrow" introduces for the first time to the West a remarkable Japanese poet in the lineage of those unconventional haiku poets, Santoka and Shiki.

As a young man, Ozaki had a brilliant future before him. He was born at Tottori in 1885, well into the modernizing period of the Meiji Restoration, in which Japan opened herself to the frantic pursuit of all things western. It was a period of economic and territorial expansion, but — unlike the present materialistic trend — also one of passionate interest in western literature, and in particular French literature. The influence of French symbolist poetry had a liberating effect upon the composition of haiku, freeing the form from stultifying rules and traditional themes. One of the leaders of this poetic reform movement was Kawahigashi Hekigodo, who broke the archaic and rigid form of the haiku in impressionist sketches like:

> The red
> Then the white
> Camellia flowers fell.

In 1911, with Ogiwara Seisensui, who was to become a great influence on Hosai, he published a magazine of revolutionary haiku called "Piled-up Clouds". The poems were in free form, without a "season word." Seisensui was inspired at first by the epigrams of Goethe and the poems of Schiller.

Ozaki Hosai was an outstanding student at school and at the prestigious Tokyo Imperial University, where he studied law but showed a preference for philosophy, in particular the teachings of Lao-Tse. After graduation, he seems to have suffered some sentimental disappointment, which may have been at the root of his future troubles.

In 1912 he began a career in various insurance agencies,

which were just then beginning to be developed in Japan. He was posted first to Osaka, then to Tokyo, but the mediocrity and narrow-mindedness of his professional colleagues began to accentuate his pessimism and a tendency towards alcoholism. Hosai's sensitivity would not allow him to enter into the aggressive world of Japanese business, with its strict codes and crushing conventions that — as they still do today — cannot admit any form of individualism or independence of mind. However, modernization had brought increasing social turmoil, from which Hosai wanted to escape by resigning his position and becoming the guardian of a temple. He had already realized that he would always be an outsider.

He became so addicted to alcohol that he would often arrive drunk at the office in the morning. His behaviour became more and more eccentric. In 1920, he left the insurance company, and took a similar post in Korea, then under Japanese domination. But drink here again proved his downfall, and he went further afield, to Manchuria, also in the hands of the Japanese, but this project was also a failure. He returned, sick with pleurisy, to Tokyo in 1923, just as the city was ravaged by the great earthquake that killed thousands.

Hosai gave up all attempts to integrate himself in Japanese society, and from then on became a wanderer, separating from his wife who had given him no child, leaving behind house and home and in the style of the Chinese classic poets taking to the road as a vagabond *haïjin*. At Kyoto, he entered a small temple, Ittoen, hoping to fortify his spirit and his body by becoming a monk. But the life was too hard for him: reading the sutras at dawn, cleaning the toilets, weeding the gardens, carrying heavy loads, doing little jobs in inns and hospitals — a life without warmth or comfort that in the severe Kyoto winters was particularly trying for his frail health. So he once again had to give up and move on to a smaller temple.

It was here, in Kyoto, that in April, 1924 Hosai learnt of the deaths of his wife and his mother. But one of the deciding events of his life took place then: he was re-united with his old school friend, the haiku poet Ogiwara Seisensui, who had also been badly mauled by life. Hosai decided to become a devotee of "the way of haiku." On that auspicious day, he and Seisensui celebrated their reunion in a colossal drinking spree, during which Hosai insulted the abbot of the temple who at once expelled him and his friend.

Hosai moved on to Kōbe, to another temple at Suma, where he wrote some of his best haiku, full of melancholy regret and an often grim humour, in which he expressed his utter loneliness and sense of abandonment by life in images of precise, brilliantly observed realism.

He again was involved in a quarrel and left Suma in 1925. After a brief stay in Kyoto with Seisensui, he left in August 1925 for the little island of Shodo in the Inland Sea, where he became the sole occupant of the Nango hermitage near the Saiko Temple. He led there the solitary existence of a hermit poet, depending solely on the offerings of strangers and temple worshippers. Here he finally achieved some degree of happiness, for his reclusive life helped him to overcome some of the deep hatred he had of men and society, a hatred that was turned against himself. His solitary existence liberated him from that tenacious detestation and ingrown misanthropy.

But he was suffering, like Shiki, from the disease of the century — tuberculosis. Seisensui wrote urging him to enter hospital, but Hosai replied: "If they make me leave my retreat, I shall refuse to eat anything and I shall die... Hospitalization? A hospital is a gloomy place, with no liberty of movement full of agitation and noise no better than cheap drink shops at festivals... But if the noise were the only thing... I have reached the point where I desire death... I've no more appetite. Hosai no longer wants to be part of 'human society'... To die, all alone, in the midst of nature, in silence... That is my dearest wish..."

This letter was written a fortnight before his death. It reveals a sort of masochistic death-wish as a disguise for suicide: or so one might think. But for Hosai this period of self-purification allowed him to unleash all his rancour and rage, and his hatred of human beings, in order to achieve peace.

His final poem, written just before he died on April 7, 1926, may be regarded as an example of the classical Chinese "death poem": it is scribbled on a scrap of rough paper:

> Springtime in the hills —
> Behind them, a column of smoke
> has begun to rise.

This final poem illustrates well his concept of poetry and the way is should be written:

"One should compose as if, with a detached mind and an empty head, one was projecting from deep inside oneself an interior song. Make poetry spontaneously, express one's feelings without restraint."

In other words, "Speak out."

The editors end their excellent introduction thus:

"Poetry is an unceasing struggle towards attaining an equilibrium between oneself and the world. In Japan there is a powerful current of popular tradition that sees in poetry a remedy against the pains and trials of life here below. If poetry is a medicine, Hosai's ultimate haiku is not a final swan-song, but the first poem of a larger work whose completion we are forever deprived of."

Hosai is indeed the supreme Japanese example of the individual at odds with a society that does not recognize individuality — the kind of society of material success and financial double-dealing that exists not only in Japan. Hosai seems to me a brother in misfortune, one of the many precursors of contemporary existential anxiety in a hard and cruel world where poets are increasingly becoming an extinct species.

An old Japanese proverb says: "A nail that sticks up must be hammered down" — that is, individualists must be made to conform. Hosai has a few haiku about nails — all bent ones that refuse to be beaten down:

> The nails
> in the nail-box
> are all bent

113

A SELECTION OF HAIKU BY OZAKI HOSAI

Evening —
a one-legged sparrow
hobbling along

The Tokyo Years : 1916-1919

trotting horse
jingling bells
city lights

The fishmonger
bellows the names of each fish
in the sun

At the florist's
a sound of scissors
I have a long lie-in

From each warship
re-echoing
morning bugle call

Angry with my wife
in the heat of the day
I walked out of the house

Seoul (Korea) and Changchun (Manchuria) : 1923

Profoundly lonely —
just to see someone,
I make my shadow move

Broad daylight   a fire
distant clouds of smoke
winter and its rows of trees

A runaway horse
a thick carpet
of white frost

114

Through the fence
the dog looks at me
and turns away

Kyoto : 1923-1924

A cockerel looks over
my shoulder at a letter
I write lying down

The beach
suddenly before me
as if it were someone

Dead leaves
stupid faces
twisted with laughter

Kōbe: the Suma Temple : 1924-1925

Not a word
all day long
butterfly shadow

In the shadow of
the Buddhist altar that radiance
of a bowl of rice — and mosquitoes

Evening —
a one-legged sparrow
hobbling along

Far from me
the criticisms of others
I shell peas

In the rice-field stubble
I saw quite close
a crow's head

All sliding doors
closed and the room
is total solitude

115

Hammered in crooked
a nail
bends its head

Like a falsehood
in broad daylight
the moon

Silken whisper
of bamboo leaves
I miss people

Heavy snowfall
all you can see of a rabbit
are his red eyes

On the seashore
however often I turn round
I can see no footprints

Knocking against a bell —
as I move away
it sounds again

In my two hands
a little warmth —
the sparrow I release

Funerary monument
so heavy
someone under there

In time with the gong
and the prayer chants
night descending

So lonely —
just to see something
I spread my five fingers

Hanging on a nail
the wet towel
frozen stiff this morning

At the memory
of a detested face
I give a pebble a kick

There is nothing
in my desk drawer
I open it and look in.

Obama: Joko Temple in Fukui : 1925

A train passing behind me
I go on pulling weeds
without lifting my head

The nails
in the nail-box
are all bent

Sparrow on the tatami
I recognize the sound
of your steps.

Nango Hermitage, Shōdoshima : 1925-1926

On the wall the newspaper
picture of a woman
is still crying

He points out the road for me
with the stem of his pipe
with smoke coming out

However much I look
through a hole in the paper door
still no one there

Even if I cough
I'm still
all alone

Under my shrunken
flesh
my thick bones

Tomorrow
first day of the year
for Buddha and me

Little island
where I live
snow on my island

Not even a visit from
a debt-collector —
lonely New Year's Eve

Spring at last!
Big headline
in the newspaper

So round, the moon
looking through
the window

Dragonfly
on my empty desk —
it was for me you came

I put down
my teacup
attack of coughing

I am very ill
a weeping willow
given to the wind

Springtime in the hills —
behind them, a column of smoke
has begun to rise.

(Translated and adapted by James Kirkup from the versions of
Makoto Kemmoku and Alain Kervern).

EPILOGUE

The Mystical Poet Tramp Santōka Taneda

A poet often feels a deep brotherhood with certain poets of the past. In my own case, I always loved Marlowe, Clare, Blake, Emily Dickinson, Baudelaire, Rimbaud. Of course, to feel an affinity with a certain poet does not mean that one's own work will be the same as his — as good or as enduring. But for a translator of poetry in particular, such an affinity is a precious asset in reaching deep into the heart and soul of his subject.

When I began reading Chinese and Japanese poets in various European language translations — long before I ever dreamed of going to live and work in the Far East — I at once sensed brotherhood with some of them. These were Han Shan, the author of the Cold Mountain poems, Wang Wei, Tu Fu and Li Po among the Chinese; and Bashō, Busan and Issa among the Japanese. I liked their way of looking at life through eyes unclouded by prejudice or by normal social ties. I, too, was a lonely wanderer in the world, without family, friends or fixed abode. Those old oriental poets spoke to me more closely than any English ones.

In Japan, I first came to admire more than any other writer Osamu Dazai, so much so that I made several visits to his grave and felt a kind of permanent regret that I had not lived in Japan during his lifetime, when I might have met him and spoken to him. The only other writers I ever felt so strongly about having missed in real life were Ronald Firbank and Robert Walser.

Then I started reading the poems of Ryōkan and Santōka, two Japanese poets whose life was poetry and whose poetry was life, both homeless wanderers, both unaffected, unpretentious seekers after the truth within themselves. In the case of Santōka, the feeling of kinship is almost unbearably strong, as if on his death in October, 1940 some of his spirit had entered into me. It was in October 1940 that I was condemned, as a conscientious objector to conscription and war, to work in a British labour camp. I was to spend the next six years in such camps, working as a forester and a farm labourer in various parts of England. It was a hard, boring, comfortless existence, but it awakened my heart to the poetry of unsentimental nature and the lonely visions of the excluded.

I think Santōka experienced life and poetry as I learned to do, through hardship, solitude and close contact with the struggles of the natural world, the sorrows of man and beast. In addition, I had (and still have) an inborn fear of my fellow countrymen: the British are the most terrifying race on earth. In such a state of morbid anguish and loneliness, an outcast from society in a Britain that was totally alien to me in its war hysteria, poetry was my salvation, and my one true companion. Through the writing of poetry, I could be myself, and accept my fate, as Santōka did. Santōka had his Zen Buddhist monk's iron begging bowl. I did not have even that: poetry was my begging bowl. The only one to put anything in it was myself. The world I saw around me was one of war-torn cities and fiery ruins, a world of blood endlessly, uselessly spilled — as it is still being spilled today. It was the sort of world Santōka was experiencing in the last years of his life, and is evoked in some of his best haiku:

The air raid sirens piling it on — red persimmons

This moon's brilliance — wonder where they are bombing now

Feet and hands left in China — bones returned to Japan

I sought refuge in the smallest things of everyday life, training my attention to perceive messages in a blade of grass, a pebble, a drop of water. I did not know it at the time, but I was following Santōka's precept: "Truth is seeing the new in the ordinary... There are treasures concealed deep in the present moment."

Moreover, in a world at war, in a land that I experienced as a cruel prison, I was able, through poetry, to construct the life I wanted. Because I had discovered, too, that there was no place, and no situation, in which I could not think of my poetry, and write it in my head as I laboured in the fields.

Santōka had been born into a prosperous middle-class family that fell on evil days with the suicide of his mother when he was

120

eleven, and the business failures of his father. After trying a few part-time jobs, he took to the road in a life of almost perpetual wandering, often in the direst poverty. In a Japan gearing for another useless war, he was an outcast whose only consolations were sakè and haiku — an existence that became one long walking Zen meditation. The depth of his despair was such that one day he put himself in the path of an express train that managed to stop just in time. He was conducted to a nearby temple, where he was taken in charge by one of his few friends, Gian Michizuki Oshō the head priest of Hōon-ji Temple, who fed him and gave him shelter without comment or question. Through Gian, Santōka learnt to be a Buddhist priest, and devised his own way of Zen, which was already in his poetry — no duplicity, pretence or superfluity — the Zen of pure experience.

Santōka had started by writing formal haiku. But after meeting the great free-style haiku poet Seisensui, began using that sparse, stripped-down form himself. He continued writing in this way until his death. His haiku were written in such plain, simple language — sometimes very down-to-earth — that they are easily translated. The difficult thing for a translator is to breathe into his versions some of that essential spirit of the poet which I sense from my first reading of his work. As Santōka wrote most of his haiku, or rather composed them in his mind while walking, they have a natural rhythm, the stresses of the human body in motion, and can be defined in the poet's own words; "One breath, one step, one line". So the haiku of Santōka have their own organic shape, which cannot be expressed properly in the normal three-line form of 5-7-5 syllables in which haiku are usually printed in the western world. Therefore I have adopted the original Japanese one-line form.

The guiding principle within all Santōka's work is one of self-purification: "Muddy water — flowing makes it run clear" means that through walking and writing his spirit and heart become cleansed of their daily impurities. And that can only be accomplished by going one's own way:

This is my one way — to walk alone.

The fine modern Japanese novelist Maruya Saiichi has written a sort of biographical mystery story about Santōka's life: *Yokoshigure,** which means driving rain — an image of which Santōka was fond. as a permanent wanderer in the mountains and fields and along the sea-coasts of Japan he encountered all kinds of rain, and all kinds of weathers of the soul, and they appear in the haiku that follow.

* *Yokoshigure*, Kodansha 1975, can be found translated into French in *L'Ombre des arbres* translated by Aude Fieschi, editions Phillippe Piquier, Paris 1993: and into English in *Rain in the Wind*, translated by Dennis Keene, Kodansha International, Tokyo 1990. Also recommended: a brief life and selection of haiku by Santōka in *Mountain Tasting* by John Stevens, Weatherall, Tokyo 1980.

HAIKU BY SANTŌKA TANEDA

My home town in the rain — walking barefoot

Walking with a dragonfly perched on my *kasa*[†]

Well now — has my *kasa* also started leaking?

I shall leave now, with my back getting wet in winter drizzle

The road so straight it makes me feel lonesome

Pushing my way pushing my way through still more green
[mountains

Even in the iron begging bowl the hailstones

Bearing the scorching sun I set out begging

In the pine tree wind I strike the temple bell every dawn and dusk

Collecting rain — one bucketful — enough for today

All damp with morning dew, I go wherever I want to

A sound of waves through winter drizzle — darkness

My iron begging bowl received one leaf falling from a tree

Stretching my legs my feet touched the man next to me —
[from Shikoku

The giant camphor tree and I and a dog getting wet
[in winter drizzle

Divided by a wall men and women in the hot bath
[all talking merrily

Sunlight falls full and free upon my freshly-shaven pate

I follow in the steps of the wind's light and shade

Hot spring — daybreak — alone, warming myself up

All day long I uttered no word — the sound of waves

My sutra chanting helpless against the noise of jazz

Lying in the grass waiting for my breech clout to get dry

This moon's brilliance — I wonder where they are bombing now

[†] A mendicant monk's laquered wickerwork hat.

123

Air-raid siren piling it on – red persimmons

I wish I could have one cup of sakè – red sunset skies

Just sitting alone and quiet in the mosquito net, eating my rice

Horse, horse, horses going to the front tomorrow face face faces

The endless night – all night long the barking of dogs

No money no food no teeth and alone

Looking down on village still sleeping as I piss

Feet and hands left in China – bones returned to Japan

So glad to be alive – newborn baby opening and
                              [closing his hands

Getting late – a cooler moon appearing between buildings

Deep mid-day – deep in grass, sounds of frog being
                              [swallowed by a snake

Blowing in the wind – my contradictions – just can't help
                              [myself

At dusk – sound of a pitiful letter being dropped in the post box

Sound of waves – now far off, now near — how many
                              [days left to me?

Pissing red urine – how long can I go on with this journey?

Cunts and cocks all together in the gushing hot spring

I just can't stop drinking sakè – trees sprouting, grass sprouting

Selling my rags for sakè – somehow still feeling sorry

The house I was born in gone without trace – fireflies flitting

***

Now I shall end this essay with one of my own one-line haiku
that curiously resembles the feeling in Santōka's "This is my one
way — to walk alone".

I follow no path — the path follows me

124

BASHŌ AND KEATS

" Beauty is truth, truth beauty" — that is all
Ye know on earth, and all ye need to know.

(Ode on a Grecian Urn)

When we read Keats' poetry and his letters, we often find him talking about "Beauty" as an almost abstract entity, and nearly always with a capital "B". He certainly had a strong appreciation of all things beautiful, but sometimes the word seemed to lead him astray into fanciful conceits and to the creation of "Poesy" rather than poetry. It seems to me that when Keats was not thinking about Beauty in the abstract, with a capital "B", he was able to write his finest verse.

We do not usually think of Keats as a realist poet, or one who seized upon sudden flashes of experience in an impressionistic manner. Yet from time to time, among all the radiantly rich tapestries of his descriptions, we find small details of keen observation that make us wish he had written more often in that manner, as in these lines from "The Eve of St. Agnes":

The hare limped trembling through the frozen grass...

which is a striking visual cameo. Its compactness makes it instantly memorable, as in the slightly larger picture contained in these lines:

Out went the taper as she hurried in;
Its little smoke, in pallid moonshine, died...

And from the same great poem, this startling image:

And the long carpets rose along the dusty floor...

Beauty is in those lines, and all the finer for being beauty with a small "b". In 1682, at a period of great trials in his life Bashō wrote this:

What is important is to keep our mind high in the world of true understanding, and returning to the world of our daily experience to seek therein the truth of beauty. No matter what we may be doing at a given moment, we

125

must not forget that it has a bearing upon our everlasting self which is poetry.

Bashō came from Iga-Ueno, near Nagoya. The Toda family ruled the area, and Bashō's father was a *samurai* in the family's service. So it was natural that Bashō should become a page or study-companion to Yoshitada, the young heir, who was two years older than Bashō, and they became firm friends. The early death of his friend was a terrible blow to Bashō, and may have contributed to the frequent themes of loneliness and sadness in his work.

A similar sense of desolation must have afflicted Keats on the death of his young brother Tom. Bashō's "the truth of beauty" is a concept linked to reality, not as in Keats' case to notions about what Beauty with a capital "B" should be. Nevertheless, the germ of Bashō's idea is also present in Keats' thought, and now and then comes out in his poetry. In his charming sonnet, "To my Brothers", we find a reference to that younger brother Tom, whose early death created a sense of deep personal loss similar to Bashō's. The sonnet opens with these realistic images:

Small, busy flames play through the fresh-laid coals,
    And their faint cracklings o'er our silence creep...

and goes on to this plain, affectionate statement:

This is your birthday, Tom, and I rejoice
    That thus it passes smoothly, quietly...

We remember that Tom was dying of tuberculosis, and that he died about three years before Keats' death from the same disease. Moreover, that year, 1818, was the one in which Keats was deeply distressed by a virulent review of his poetry in *Blackwood's Edinburgh Magazine* – "Back to the shop, Mr. John, back to plasters, pills and ointment boxes." Fellow poets in Britain are often the most vengeful and spiteful of creatures, and Byron was no exception, for he wrote of "Johnny Keats' piss-a-bed poetry". Shelley was convinced that Keats had been killed by his critics. A poet has to be tough to survive in a hostile world.

126

The lines I have quoted from "To my Brothers" are of singular simplicity, but they are true poetry. There are similar simple, deft observations of nature in "I Stood tip-toe upon a Little Hill":

A bush of may flowers with the bees about them...

A filbert hedge with wild briar overtwined...

These are images that a haiku poet would have made. In a letter to Benjamin Robert Haydon, Keats writes of "that tremblingly delicate and snail-horn perception of Beauty." The beauty again has a capital, which seems excessive when applied to the humble snail that is a favourite image in haiku poetry. However, poetic perception is not always so "delicate" and the realism of some haiku is often startlingly down-to-earth. Nevertheless, a certain delicacy of touch is required to make the best of a brief poem of seventeen syllables. Keats is at the opposite extreme of poetic creation when he says: "Poetry should surprise by a fine excess" and his advice to Shelley was: "Load every rift of your subject with ore". But it is not the way a haiku poet works: his technique is to strip everything down to the essentials, to essences, and to keep a firm hand on his emotions, letting the plain words speak for themselves, without comment.

Like John Keats in his letters, Bashō often expresses profound thoughts about the poetic life and the making of verse. That old pond into which the famous frog jumped is like the mirror of the poetic mind, so calm, so still, yet capable of being suddenly animated by the inspiration of an unexpected event, the flash of a new vision of the ordinary, or even some accident of composition. Bashō wrote:

Go to the pine if you want to learn about the pine, or the bamboo if you want to learn about the bamboo. And in doing so, you must leave behind your subjective preoccupation with yourself, otherwise you impose yourself on the object and do not learn. Your poetry issues of its own accord when you and your subject have become one – when you have plunged deep enough into the object to see something like a glimmering there.

> However well phrased your poetry may be, if your
> feeling is not natural – if the object and yourself are
> separate – then your poetry is not true poetry but merely
> your subjective conterfeit.

I think those wise words of Bashō apply to whatever kind of poem one is trying to write, in whatever language. They can be applied to forms as different as the epic and the epigram, for I believe all true poetry is a perception of essences. This is particularly true of such a tough, taut yet infinitely pliable form as the haiku. I wish Keats had been able to read those lines. I am sure he would have appreciated them and learnt from them. But Bashō could also have learned from Keats.

What did Keats say? "Poetry should be great and unobtrusive, a thing which enters into one's soul, and does not startle or amaze it with itself, but with its subject."

This refreshing immediacy in Keats' apprehension of the nature of poetry can be parallelled with Bashō's statement:

> When composing a verse let there not be a hair's breadth
> separating your mind from what you write. Composition
> of a poem must be done in an instant, like a woodcutter
> felling a huge tree or a swordsman leaping at a dangerous
> enemy.

Bashō would certainly have approved of another of Keats' sayings: "If poetry comes not as naturally as the leaves to a tree, it had better not come at all." That seems to be exactly what Bashō meant in his advice that we should plunge deeply into the subject, to find its secret, glimmering essence. And he himself might have been speaking when Keats says: "We hate poetry that has a palpable design upon us... Poetry should be great and unobtrusive..."

But "unobtrusive" is hardly the word we should apply to some of Keats' greatest works. The "Ode to Autumn" is great precisely as a structure of carefully-counted syllabic lines arranged in a definite and willed pattern in which the rhyme scheme is intimately linked to the syllabic content. Even the indentations at the beginning of each line correspond to the syllabic and rhyme patterns, that never vary throughout the three verses of eleven lines each – perhaps an unconscious link with the eleventh month of the year, when autumn is at its peak. But the sensuous beauty and rich diversity of the poet's imagery together with the pure passion of his emotion could never be called "unobtrusive" – and no one would expect it to be so:

Season of mists and mellow fruitfulness,
    Close bosom-friend of the maturing sun;
Conspiring with him how to load and bless
    With fruit the vines that round the thatch-eves run;
To bend with apples the moss'd cottage-trees,
    And fill all fruit with ripeness to the core;
      To swell the gourd, and plump the hazel shells
With a sweet kernel; to set budding more,
And still more, later flowers for the bees,
Until they think warm days will never cease,
    For summer has o'er-brimm'd their clammy cells.

The most unobtrusive thing in this poem is the very tight technical construction: one has to deliberately count every syllable and measure the relationship of lines, indentations and rhymes to the general syllabic pattern to discover the hidden secret of the poem's success. For the poet is in full control of his form, and this purely technical discipline, which he must have worked very hard to obtain, keeps the very lush, very obtrusive imagery firmly in place.

There is the way a traditional haiku poet works, counting his syllables and arranging his season words in the style of the old masters, so often condemned and rejected by modern versifiers. A correct Japanese haiku about autumn would contain only one season word, with perhaps a minor, secondary reference if necessary. And yet the true haiku would express a certain essence of the season in that one reference to it.

There is something of Bashō's feeling for the wildness of the "deep north" of Tohoku in another letter of Keats, in which he says: "The roaring of the wind is my wife and the stars through the window are my children." This reminds us of Sora's haiku towards the end of *Oku no Hosomichi* (The Narrow Road to the Deep North), which Bashō recorded, presumably because it expressed his own feelings of loneliness and desolation at Zenshōji Temple, "near the castle of Daishōji in the province of Kaga":

> Hearing all night long
> autumn wind in the mountain
> behind the temple

In many of Bashō's most original and realistic writings, we are again and again reminded of Keats, who wrote: "A poet is the most unpoetical of anything in existence because he has no identity – he is continually informing and filling some other body." Some other body – yes, the poet has to keep getting under the skin of his subjects. Bashō writes about the beauties of nature in a fairly conventional way, but also about things many people in Keats' day might have found unpoetical – fleas, lice, horses pissing, drunkenness, cucumbers, clam shells, an old fan scribbled with haiku. Yet the "Ode to Autumn" is abuzz with insects, and one of my favourite Keats sonnets, "On the Grasshopper and the Cricket" is full of pure haiku feeling.

On the evening of December 30, 1816, when Keats and Charles Cowden Clarke were visiting Leigh Hunt in Hampstead, the last-named, inspired by the cricket that was singing beside the fireplace, suggested that he and Keats have a sonnet-writing contest on the subject of the grasshopper and the cricket. Hunt started his sonnet in a very haikuesque manner: "Green little vaulter in the sunny grass..." Keats' opening line is one of his simplest and greatest:

> The poetry of earth is never dead:
>> When all the birds are faint with the hot sun,
>> And hide in cooling trees, a voice will run
> From hedge to hedge about the new-mown mead;
> That is the Grasshopper's – he takes the lead
>> In summer luxury, – he has never done
>> With his delights; for when tired out with fun
> He rests at ease beneath some pleasant weed.

The poetry of earth is ceasing never:
    On a lone winter evening, when the frost
Has wrought a silence, from the stove there shrills
The Cricket's song, in warmth increasing ever,
    And seems to me in drowsiness half lost
The Grasshopper's among the grassy hills.

A similar haikuesque feeling informs "Sleep and Poetry":

Stop and consider! Life is but a day;
A fragile dew-drop on its perilous way
From a tree's summit...

That corresponds to the Japanese sense of the fleetingness of human existence expressed in all the arts, but particularly in haiku, in which the song of the cicada sometimes has the poignancy of the grasshopper or the cricket. Bashō has two famous haiku about cicadas:

Cicadas singing –
stridulations drill the rocks –
how quiet it is

and

Listening to them,
it's hard to believe they'll soon
be dead – the cicadas

Bashō also wrote about the grasshopper's chirping:

What pathetic sounds –
grasshoppers chirping under
broken war-helmets

Bashō demonstrates the truth of Keats' words in one of his last letters: "The only means of strengthening one's intellect is to make up one's mind about nothing – to let the mind be a thoroughfare for all thoughts." The poetic mind has to be open continually for the reception of new images, and this openness can best be achieved by wandering among the thoroughfares of human existence, to be free of all attachments so that poems, and haiku, may flow unfettered. This non-attachment is one of the first

131

principles of Zen Buddhism, a principle that the agnostic side of Keats, one might almost say his paganism, accepted instinctively. One senses a certain note of relief at the ending of his attachment to Fanny Brawne.

Bashō writes in *The Records of a Travelworn Satchel*: "From this day forth/ I shall be called a wanderer..." And: "With a bit of madness in me which is poetry..."

Makoto Ueda, in *Zaemi, Bashō, Yeats, Pound* (Mouton, The Hague, 1965), tells us that Bashō's ideal life was, in his own words, "to enjoy life by being indifferent to worldly interests, by forgetting whether one is young or old." As he grew older, the loneliness that afflicts mosts artists in some way or other became even more acute, so that in his short essay, "On a Life of Solitude", we read:

> Indolent old man that I am, finding visitors irksome, I often determine not to go and see my friends or to ask them to come to me: and yet I cannot help longing for them on moon-lit evenings and snowy mornings. For on a night of snow, I have to drink sakè in silence, having none but myself to ask questions and none but myself to answer them. From time to time I open the sliding windows to view the snow, and then I sit down to drink more sakè. I take my writing brush in my hand, and after writing a little, lay it down. What a restless old man I am!

This passage reminds us of his haiku, composed at his solitary retreat, the Bashō-an in what was then a fairly remote part of Edo, Fukagawa:

> Drinking sakè, I
> grow ever more wakeful on
> this night of snowfall

This haiku conveys very well the sense of *yugen* or "loneliness with resignation". This feeling is one of the most persuasive and moving in Bashō's work. It is the exact mood of Keats' "La Belle Dame Sans Merci":

> O what can ail thee, knight-at-arms,
>   Alone and palely loitering?

The sedge has withered from the lake,
    And no birds sing...

And this is why I sojourn here
    Alone and palely loitering,
Though the sedge is withered from the lake,
    And no birds sing.

From Kyoto I sometimes went to visit the grave of Ernest
Fennollosa at the Homyoin Temple in Hama-Otsu, and at the same
time paid homage at the grave of Bashō nearby in the grounds of
Gichuji Temple. On my last visit there, I wrote this poem in his
honour:

At the Grave of Bashō

No incense burns, old poet,
before your plain stone obelisk,
and there are no country flowers
in the bamboo jars.

A small green tree
with dark pointed foliage
and whose name I do not know
leans its shadow over you.

On the other side,
a bush with heart-shaped leaves
now in July has one leaf stained
with November red.

I plucked the leaf,
because it may have been a sign from you.
It was the only signal I could give –
a passing greeting from one wanderer to another.

I often paid homage at Keats' grave, too. Whenever I am in
Rome, I go first to the Roman Catholic cemetery, the Campo
Verano, to lay some flowers on the grave of Ronald Firbank. Then
I go to the Protestant Cemetery close to the Pyramid of Cestius, to
visit the grave of John Keats, who shortly before his death
dictated to his loyal friend Charles Brown his own epitaph:

"Here lies one whose name was writ in water."

On one of my visits, on 23 February, I realized that it was the anniversary of John Keats' tragic death in that little room above the Spanish Steps, and I was moved to see that in the late winter sunshine violets were blooming round the gravestone. I wrote in memory of a great poet not a haiku but a *tanka*, in thirty-one syllables and five lines, the poetic form from which the haiku was derived:

> The tombstone of one
> whose name was writ in water –
> his own epitaph –
> casts shadows in the spring grass
> lit by flames of violets.

(Talk delivered at Keats House, Hampstead, London on June 21, 1995)

***